The Classroom Management Handbook

A practical blueprint for engagement and behaviour in your classroom and beyond

& Oliver Lovell

Designed by Jamie Clark

JOHN CATT
FROM HODDER EDUCATION

Orders: please contact Hachette UK Distribution, Hely Hutchinson Centre, Milton Road, Didcot, Oxfordshire, OX11 7HH. Telephone: +44 (0)1235 827827. Email education@hachette.co.uk. Lines are open from 9 a.m. to 5 p.m., Monday to Friday.

ISBN: 9781398388437

© Mark Dowley & Oliver Lovell 2024

First published in 2024 by
John Catt from Hodder Education,
An Hachette UK Company
15 Riduna Park, Station Road,
Melton, Woodbridge IP12 1QT

www.johncatt.com

To my family. Thanks for providing me unwavering support, friendship, and love.

- Mark

To Holly. Thanks for your constant love, support, and encouragement.

And for always keeping me in line!

- Ollie

CONTENTS

ACKNOWLEDGEMENTS

MARK DOWLEY

I am eternally grateful to the experts who have written books and taught behaviour management. The ideas within this book build on the great work done by master teachers and behaviour management experts including Bill Rogers, Peter Myles, Tom Bennett and Doug Lemov. A particular thank you to Dr. Jim Knight for demonstrating the power of conversations to build relationships with students and colleagues.

Thank you to Brighton Grammar for the opportunity to work with so many amazing teachers. Thank you to all my colleagues who have allowed me to visit classes during my career and the coaches who have helped me hone my classroom management skills. A special thank you to Dr. Ray Swann for his contributions on culture and the W.I.N. conversational model (found in Routine 6) and Bryn Humberstone, especially for contributing the ideas that underpin the following tools: show you're equitable, offer expectant help and addressing rough play (found in Routines 12 and 13). Thank you to Ollie for his essential guidance on the art of writing. This book would not exist without you sharing your knowledge and processes for writing and editing. Also, thank you for the way you challenge my thinking, literally every day, and for allowing me to become a better educator. I'm grateful to have you as a colleague and friend.

I am so thankful to the educators who read drafts and gave valuable feedback: Kristen Molloy, Jessica Colleau-Terradas, Emma Egan, Luke Casserly, Deeana Audino, Jarret Tracey, Brian Dowley and Emily Henderson. This book is better because of your support.

Thank you to all the students who have been in our classes who make teaching such an interesting, challenging and rewarding profession.

OLLIE LOVELL

I owe an enormous debt of gratitude to all the educators who have come before and written and taught on classroom and behaviour management. I was lucky enough to have Bill Rogers give a lecture to my class during my initial teacher education, and that was the first time that my eyes were opened to the fact that there are structured and systematic things that teachers can do to manage student behaviour.

Having Bill on the *Education Research Reading Room* podcast further initiated a leap in my personal knowledge of classroom management strategies, and having Tom Bennett and Doug Lemov on the podcast too provided further and richer knowledge on how norms and routines can have phenomenal impacts in the classroom and make more time for the core business of teaching and learning.

It was also Bill Rogers who initially alerted me to the importance of teachers planning their language, which has since evolved into the structured script-based approach that forms the basis of much of this book. I'm also grateful to Josh Goodrich and the Steplab team for really raising my awareness about the crucial role of rehearsal to turning teaching aspirations into habits, and to truly driving sustainable change.

A massive thanks goes to Brighton Grammar for their support of Mark and my explorations of these important issues. Thanks to Bryn Humberstone for being a particular model of quality classroom management (and school yard management). I've learned a lot from Bryn on student management during our time together.

This book wouldn't exist without the fantastic work of Dr. Mark Dowley in driving the project forward. Mark has done the hard work of constantly bringing me back to this important project, despite my many competing commitments, and has kept us on track and focused along the way. It's been a joy mulling over and co-developing the ideas herein with him, and I'm grateful to be able to share an office and so many fantastic projects with Mark.

Finally, thanks to my family, Holly, Ada, Madeleine, Malcolm and Elliott, for being a constant source of support and encouragement, and for your continuous understanding of my passion for education.

FOREWORD

BILL ROGERS

With refreshing honesty, informed by their years of teaching, Ollie and Mark begin this book by sharing their own natural challenges they have faced in behaviour leadership and teaching engagement. When we chose this profession, we can all remember the natural struggle coming to terms with how best to lead for behaviour and learning with our students: what should we do, and why (the value question)? And also (the utility question), what and how? This book securely addresses these crucial questions.

Ollie and Mark have developed a text that comprehensively addresses how best to address behaviour and learning in a wide range of contexts and covering the common issues that we all face as teachers day after day. This book is well researched and is immediately and crucially practical and meaningful in what it outlines as best practice. Most of all, it is securely grounded in our teaching reality.

The handbook is divided into two parts. Part 1 sets out the core principles for effective classroom management. These principles are foundational for the way we lead for behaviour and learning.

Part 2 outlines 18 crucial routines, grounded in practical specificity at the level of language we use to lead for behaviour, learning and encouragement. As the authors note, they have sought to 'distil the most practical and high impact teaching strategies' in their book. They affirm, as I do, they have seen these strategies at work in the widest range of teaching and schooling contexts. In the second part of this book, Mark and Ollie pay particular attention to the significance of our language when we lead for behaviour and learning. It is encouraging to see this issue explored in this text. This is a crucial and commendable feature of this handbook.

We are not always aware of how we characteristically lead for distracting and disruptive behaviour. This is another notable strength of this book, which encourages reflection on our characteristic behaviour leadership language in the light of the common issues we face in the classroom and in the playground. The aim of such language cueing is to enable students to be aware of their behaviour and to take ownership of that behaviour in a way that considers the rights of others.

The authors have given us a framework of language that can balance the need to address a range of distracting and disruptive behaviours; to do so within the context of 25+ students in a classroom and with humanity and respect is no mean feat.

Ollie and Mark emphasise several times in the text that teaching is deeply human work. As the eminent psychiatrist Alfred Adler noted, we all have a central, social need to belong. As you read these principles and practices and the language cues and exchanges between teachers and students, you will note this axiom central to our profession.

This book will repay careful reading by those who have taken on a demanding and a crucial profession.

I avidly commend this book to any teacher, whether you're beginning your teaching journey or whether you are a senior colleague in our profession. This is certainly an essential book to enable those wanting to reflect on their characteristic behaviour, leadership and management. It would form an invaluable foundation for professional development in this area. Most of all it will encourage and remind you of why you chose to be a teacher.

Kind regards and best wishes,

Bill Rogers

Bill Rogers is an education consultant,
author and founder of the Rogers Education Consultancy.

INTRODUCTION

MY FIRST DAY – MARK DOWLEY

It was a hot summer day in a rural town. With the nervous energy and optimism that comes from being a new teacher, I walked towards my first ever class – Year 9 physical education. In my head, I was ready. I had planned one of the most fun and engaging classes you could imagine. We were learning about motor skills and there was no better way to introduce it than to give the students not one but four fun activities to work through in a circuit. With basketball, tennis, cricket and football, everyone was sure to be engaged... right?

The moment I began speaking, it slowly started to unravel. Some students weren't listening. I spoke a bit louder. 'Surely they'll figure it out once the activities start' – I naively thought to myself. After ten minutes of ignored explanations, I told students they could start the activities. But they didn't start well. The footballers were kicking balls at the basketball ring, I hadn't planned for that. We were losing tennis balls over the fence at an unsustainable rate. I used my whistle to try to create some order, I found myself yelling, something I associated with grumpy teachers who were 'past it'. The existential questions began: 'Have I made the wrong decision to be a teacher?' 'Am I cut out for this?' After 50 painful minutes, I was saved by the bell. The students dispersed (laughing, they'd had a great time) whilst I sat down, dejected, flustered, exhausted, and already worried about the next lesson.

Teaching, I had just discovered, is hard!

With time, I learned that this was not an isolated experience. Classroom management is complex and many teachers find it challenging. Over 75% of teachers report that disruption and disengagement occur 'almost daily', 'daily' or 'several times a day'.[1] These disruptive behaviours include avoiding work, talking, moving around the room, using phones, or being late to class. It's also a nationwide problem, as the OECD's disciplinary climate index shows, my home country of Australia ranks 70th out of 77 school systems, meaning our classrooms are among the OECD's most disorderly.[2] The situation is similar in other English-speaking countries like England, Canada and New Zealand which don't rank much better. They aren't necessarily all out of control, but it's definitely true that they just aren't productive.

Compounding this, many teachers leave the profession in the first five years, with some research suggesting this number is as high as 40–50%.[3] The primary reason cited is teacher workload, but when the concept of workload is explored, the main factors are invariably the time and energy teachers spend on student behaviour. This leads to teacher burnout and resignation.[4]

On a more encouraging note, for teachers who have positive relationships with their students and the skills required to manage a classroom effectively, teaching can be the most rewarding job in the world. There are common tools and routines that work with diverse groups of students. Even if the management isn't perfect, the same practices can definitely improve the culture in the classroom, which equates to improvements

1. Goss, P. and Sonnemann, J. (2017). *Engaging students: Creating classrooms that improve learning*. Grattan Institute.

2. OECD (2018). PISA 2018 Results (Volume III): What School Life Means for Students' Lives. www.oecd-ilibrary. org/sites/f05bb3ee-en/index.html?itemId=/content/component/f05bb3ee-en.

3. Ingersoll, R. M., Merrill, E., Stuckey, D. and Collins, G. (2018). *Seven trends: The transformation of the teaching force* [updated October 2018].

4. Carroll, A., Forrest, K., Sanders-O'Connor, E., Flynn, L., Bower, J. M., Fynes-Clinton, S., York, A. and Ziaei, M. (2022). *Teacher stress and burnout in Australia: examining the role of intrapersonal and environmental factors*. Social Psychology of Education, 25(2–3), 441–469.

in both student learning[5] and teacher satisfaction. Teaching is the most important profession and we want teachers to enjoy teaching their classes and feel energised when they walk out of the room.

The aim of this book is to share, in a simplified way, the tools and strategies of the most effective teachers. By learning and practising these skills, you'll be empowered to develop a culture of attention and learning in your classroom. This culture allows students to be engaged in learning and in their school community, which increases their chances of success later in life.

So, what happened after my first ever class? Fortunately, my mentor teacher saw me. He recommended I go to the library and borrow *You Know the Fair Rule* by Bill Rogers. That book changed the way I teach. I read it every morning over breakfast and slowly I saw my behaviour management skills improve and my classes become more productive. Then I read Rogers' other books, multiple times, followed by books from other behaviour management experts. I began sharing my learning with colleagues and they asked me to run workshops about it. Over the next 15 years, my roles included pastoral positions, curriculum leader, instructional coach, director, and associate head in a variety of schools. It culminated in Ollie and I running the *Practical Classroom Management* course at La Trobe University. In this book, we distil those experiences into the essential tools required for you to support your students.

---

5. Gill, B., Shoji, M., Coen, T. and Place, K. (2016). The content, predictive power, and potential bias in five widely used teacher observation instruments, (REL 2017–191). Washington, DC: U.S. Department of Education, Institute of Education Sciences, National Center for Education Evaluation and Regional Assistance, Regional Educational Laboratory MidAtlantic.

OLLIE LOVELL

Like Mark, I was lucky enough to come across the work of Bill Rogers early on in my teaching career. Bill came to speak to my pre-service teaching cohort at Melbourne University and his advice blew my mind. Before Bill's visit, it hadn't occurred to me that there was anything other than 1. experience, or 2. being a big burly man with a booming voice, that could help me with my classroom management.

What Bill showed me in that talk, his books, and the eventual discussion that we had in my lounge room for the *Education Research Reading Room* podcast,[6] was that there are a set of tried and tested techniques that, if learned and mastered, can support any teacher to have more success in promoting a positive and productive learning environment in their classroom. Bill first introduced me to these ideas, but there have been many since who have helped me to build this ever-expanding toolbox of tools for the classroom.

I first summarised behaviour management lessons from my discussions with the world's best educators in my second book, *Tools for Teachers*, in which I dedicated a whole chapter to the subject. Since then, I've had many, many teachers email and message me to say how much the explicit advice in that behaviour chapter has helped them with their classroom management. Knowing the value of this content to practising teachers has pushed me even further down this classroom management rabbit hole.

Since *Tools for Teachers* was released, I've spent time working with Dr. Mark Dowley to further refine the ideas in that book, to build on them and, perhaps most importantly, to expand the collection of teacher scripts that help to explicitly set teachers up for classroom management success. We have road tested these scripts and this content both with the teachers in our classroom management course through La Trobe University and our coachees, and we're confident that they offer teachers more behavioural support than ever before. As such, we're now supremely excited to be able to bring these blueprints for classroom management success to an

---

6. www.ollielovell.com/billrogers

even bigger audience through this handbook. Part 1 will share ten key principles of classroom management. Part 2 will give you the scripts and exact phrases you can use in the classroom.

We hope you find this handbook to be a trusty friend to help you with your behaviour management. Something you can keep in your jacket pocket, your school bag, or your purse, and pull out, refer to, dog ear, write on, and lean on whenever you're feeling that a little behavioural boost could help in your classroom. Do let us know how you get on with it, and good luck!

How to use this book

This book is designed as a handbook. It contains both a solid foundation in the principles of classroom management (part 1), as well as a quick reference guide to help you deal with common behaviour management scenarios (part 2).

We suggest that you read part 1, as well as the introduction to part 2 up till the end of *remember to rehearse* on page 51 from start to finish. These sections form a crucial bedrock for the ideas to come. For the remainder of part 2, the routines and scripts, we invite you to dip in and out of these as you see fit, focusing first on the scenarios that seem most important to you at the time.

Within part 2, you will notice a substantial amount of consistency, and at times repetition, between the different routines. This is because effective classroom management is essentially the use of a few core teaching tools, applied flexibly to a range of scenarios. As such, part 2 provides explicit guidance around how such tools and routines can be adapted to different scenarios. In tandem with the foundational understanding provided in part 1, these vignettes should leave you feeling confident to face many, many challenging situations in the classroom.

PART 1:
TEN PRINCIPLES FOR EFFECTIVE CLASSROOM MANAGEMENT

Expertise can be categorised as either routine or adaptive.[7] A chef with routine expertise can make a tasty meal only if they are working in a familiar kitchen, with familiar tools, and the same old ingredients. A chef with adaptive expertise, on the other hand, can make a masterpiece in any kitchen and with whatever is found in the fridge. The changing and dynamic environment of the classroom is like entering a new kitchen every day. As such, teachers need adaptive expertise, but it is practically impossible to jump straight from no expertise to adaptive expertise. This is because the expertise of the adaptive expert is built upon knowledge of thousands of recipes and experience in numerous environments over their lifetime. Thus, all expertise must begin with recipes.

That's why we provide you with recipes in the second half of this book. These recipes – in the form of scripts that you can use to address common behavioural challenges – are your tickets to quick and early behaviour management improvements. But if all we gave you were recipes, then you would likely be in trouble. Recipes alone don't build the deep and rich mental models, and the principle-based understanding, that enables an expert to truly adapt. This is why we look at principles in part 1.

---

7. Hatano, G. and Inagaki, K. (1984). Two courses of expertise. 乳幼児発達臨床センター年報, 6, 27–36.

The ten principles in part 1 represent hard-won knowledge that forms the basis of all expert classroom managers. By studying these principles and committing them to memory, you will be empowered to interpret the recipes in part 2 in a more nuanced way, and to begin to adapt them more effectively to your own context.

By way of introduction, here are those ten important principles for classroom management:

1 Cracking behaviour is cracking a code

2 The best classroom managers have the best habits

3 Beginning with high expectations provides more flexibility over time

4 Master your own behaviour to influence others

5 Behaviour is a curriculum, treat it as such

6 It's what you say and how you say it

7 Success is the greatest motivator

8 Seek out examples of excellence

9 Students need to know they belong and that you believe in them

10 Bank positivity

Once understood, these principles will form the basis of the continuing journey to true adaptive expertise.

PRINCIPLE 1:
CRACKING BEHAVIOUR IS CRACKING A CODE

Each student has a personal code that governs their behaviour. Their code is a combination of environmental, social and internal factors that must align for the student to feel safe, settled and motivated. When a student's individual code is cracked, they will behave. When it isn't, they won't. As teachers tasked with creating a focused and productive classroom environment, it's our responsibility to crack the code for every student, every lesson.

There are a broad array of tools and routines that you can and should master to become a classroom management expert. Providing you with these tools and routines is the fundamental purpose of this book. But these tools and routines won't always work the first time and, as Marder and colleagues put it: 'Teachers need to adapt their classroom management strategies to the given situation and the specific students in the classroom.'[8]

The ultimate goal of the code breaking[9] metaphor is to help you to adopt the mindset of an *adaptive* expert with respect to classroom management. By seeing yourself as a code breaker, you become more focused on the mechanisms[10] that underlie the phenomena in your classroom, and you can more flexibly deal with a wider array of students and scenarios in your classroom.[11] When you see classroom management as code breaking, you're on the path to adaptive expertise.

The code breaking metaphor has another major benefit, it's inclusive. Not every student is cast from the same mould. They each have their quirks, needs and tendencies. Some approaches will make Student A tick, whilst ticking Student B off. When we see classroom management as code breaking, we don't conclude that Student A is a good kid and that Student B is bad. Instead, we see both students as motivated by a complex combination of needs, habits and behaviours. Realising this can help us to design solutions that can make school a supportive and productive place for all students.

But don't get us wrong. This doesn't mean that each student has a wholly unique code. We're not talking about bringing cupcakes for Student A whilst allowing Student B to sit on a beanbag every lesson. We're not suggesting you reinvent the classroom management wheel for every individual student. Rather, the best place to start when it comes to code breaking is with the collection of tools that have worked to unlock many students' potential before. Luckily, the set of tools and routines that have been effective in countless classrooms before are also the ones most likely to be effective in yours.

---

8. Marder, J., Thiel, F. and Göllner, R. (2023). Classroom management and students' mathematics achievement: The role of students' disruptive behavior and teacher classroom management. *Learning and Instruction*, 86, 101746. Pg. 2.

9. This metaphor of code breaking is adapted from the domain of mental health management. See: Eastley, H. (2022, October 15). No Feeling is Final (RMIT Culture, Ed.) [Performance *No Feeling is Final*]. The Capitol, Melbourne.

10. See: Lovell, O. (2021) *Tools for Teachers,* John Catt Educational (pp. 248–252) for a detailed look into mechanisms.

11. Carbonell, K. B., Stalmeijer, R. E., Könings, K. D., Segers, M. and van Merriënboer, J. J. (2014). How experts deal with novel situations: A review of adaptive expertise. *Educational Research Review*, 12, 14–29.

These are the tools that are provided to you in this book. The 18 routines – and tools of which they are comprised – are your best bets when it comes to classroom management. But remember, you are a code breaker too. If one of the ideas suggested herein doesn't work the first time, that doesn't mean it's a broken code, or that your students are just too badly behaved. It means that there are a few digits missing that you still need to work out.

Wrangle your adaptive expertise and bring the code breaker's mindset to truly crack the challenging class.

PRINCIPLE 2:
THE BEST CLASSROOM MANAGERS
HAVE THE BEST HABITS

The best classroom managers have the best habits and habits are created through deliberate practice.

Teaching is cognitively demanding. Teachers must think about curriculum, behaviour, instruction, feedback and many other variables, all at the same time. In support of this fact, Lee S. Shulman wrote:

> 'After some 30 years… I have concluded that classroom teaching is the most demanding, subtle, nuanced, and frightening activity that our species has ever invented… the only time medicine ever approaches the complexity of an average day for a classroom teacher is in an emergency room during a natural disaster.'[12]

12. Shulman, L. S. and Wilson, S. M. (2004). *The wisdom of practice: Essays on teaching, learning, and learning to teach.* Jossey-Bass.

Compounding this challenge, all of these tasks must be simultaneously managed with our limited working memory system, which can be easily overwhelmed.[13] The only way that teachers overcome this limitation is by turning many of the routine tasks of teaching into automated habits.

As a result, every teacher has habits and those habits are formed alarmingly quickly in a teacher's career.[14] Expert teachers have automated effective routines for each part of the lesson: entry routine, settling the class, monitoring independent work, reacting to disruptions, responding to common misconceptions. Mastering and automatising these basics frees up teachers' limited working memory resources to be more adaptable, responsive and effective in new and complex situations.

For a concrete example, let's consider a novice vs. an expert teacher's mindset at the beginning of a class. A novice teacher will be thinking about where they need to stand, what they need to say, how to respond to a group of gossiping students, and what content they will need to teach. In contrast, the expert will automatically and effortlessly take their position, give clear behavioural instructions, address non-compliance, and begin the content of the lesson.

Because the expert can do all this automatically and effortlessly, they can continue to improve by building new productive habits on top of their existing routines, such as scanning the room for students who may be missing their equipment, or reading facial expressions to tune into the emotional state of their students as they enter.

To automate routines and move from novice to expert, it takes deliberate practice. Deliberate practice is the most direct and effective process for developing procedural expertise. K. Anders Ericsson describes this process in four steps:[15]

---

13. Lovell, O. (2020). *Sweller's Cognitive Load Theory In Action.* John Catt Educational.

14. Hobbiss, M., Sims, S. and Allen, R. (2021). Habit formation limits growth in teacher effectiveness: A review of converging evidence from neuroscience and social science. *Review of Education*, 9(1), 3–23.

15. Ericsson, A. and Pool, R. (2016). *Peak: Secrets from the new science of expertise.* Penguin Random House.

1. Identify keys skills that impact performance

When it comes to classroom management, the key skills are the tools and routines found in this book: entry routines, giving instructions, defusing debate, and more.

2. Develop training methods to improve those skills

Training methods are most effective when they provide the learner with opportunities to practise the key skills in relevant contexts, but in a way that approximates the real-life situation in a slightly simplified form. An example would be going to the relevant situational context, such as the classroom you are going to be teaching in, and rehearsing a classroom management routine – where you will stand, what you will say, and how you will say it, posture and tone, and so on – with a colleague providing feedback or simulating the role of the student (real-life situational context, simplified form). For best results, do this repeatedly and with feedback from an expert colleague.

3. Focus on specific goals – not vague overall performance improvements

Specific goals provide concrete targets to work towards alongside a standard by which to measure success. In terms of classroom management, specific goals could be phases of a lesson. It might be entry routines, transitions, instructional phases, independent work, group work, and so on. To make goals even more specific, they can be made concrete and measurable, for example:

- Starting routine: All students started in under 60 seconds.

- Attention signal: All students are silent, listening, with eyes forward within two seconds of the attention signal.

- Instruction: 100% of students get the final check for understanding correct prior to independent practice.

4. Work towards a series of small changes that will gradually improve performance over time

By focusing on a series of small bite-sized changes rather than rapid wholesale change, performance can be improved incrementally and sustainably, instead of risking overwhelm and a reversion to earlier and less effective habits. This could mean starting from the entry routine and ensuring students begin productively and only then focusing on the next phase of the lesson including gaining attention, followed by instruction.

The best classroom managers have the best habits and habits are created through deliberate practice. This means identifying key skills and rehearsing them in realistic contexts as you work incrementally towards specific goals. In the words of Hobbis, Sims, and Allen, 'professional development should involve repeated practice in realistic settings in order to overwrite and upgrade existing habits'.[16] The routines within this book provide you with the bite-sized goals you need, and the required blueprint of what success looks like, for you to work towards habitual classroom management mastery.

---

16. Hobbiss, M., Sims, S. and Allen, R. (2021). Ibid, pg. 1.

PRINCIPLE 3:
BEGINNING WITH HIGH EXPECTATIONS PROVIDES MORE FLEXIBILITY OVER TIME

Let us describe one of the most common scenarios we have seen when a teacher begins the year with a new class. Students are generally compliant in the first lesson, everyone is a bit nervous about being with a new group of people and the social norms aren't clear as yet. In response to this, the teacher gains a premature sense of security. The teacher progressively relaxes their standards with each lesson, at the same time as students' confidence rises and they act up more and more. Slowly, the expectations around noise and work level drop. After about six weeks, the class is more disengaged and difficult to manage. It's at this point that teachers seek help with classroom management. Unfortunately, the class norms are already established.

In contrast, master teachers begin with high expectations from day one and sustain these expectations lesson on lesson. This sets a high benchmark for student behaviour and establishes the behavioural norms required for effective learning.

One of the reasons for this pattern of the novice is that some teachers have a false dichotomy in their mind. They see a trade-off between being strict and having a good relationship with their students. In truth, strictness (or structure) and relationships are positively correlated. Strictness and structures can *support* good relationships. This is best summed up by a recent conversation with a student who was new to the school. Mark asked: 'Who is your favourite teacher?' The student replied: 'Miss White, because when she talks, all the students just listen and do what she says.' Students want the class to be well managed.

We also see examples of new teachers who often try hard to be liked by their students. A common outcome of this is that teachers focus too much on being the 'cool' teacher, and not enough time establishing high expectations. Relationships are important but, in the long run, students will most respect those teachers who lead the class to achievement, not those who let them go to break early.

Somewhat paradoxically, when a master teacher has high standards and embedded routines, it actually makes space for more complex activities and even jokes. This is because a well-behaved class can work together productively in a range of contexts and can refocus quickly and efficiently after a teacher's joke. Mark once coached a teacher who had a real knack for making amusing and lesson-relevant quips, but every time he did valuable learning time was lost bringing the class back to attention. The teacher had to stop telling jokes. Through coaching, we worked on the clarity and consistency of his signal to bring the students back to attention. Gaining the ability to bring students back to attention within two seconds opened up the space for him to be able to re-introduce his witty remarks.

Beginning with high expectations provides more flexibility over time and allows for more fun in the classroom, not less.

PRINCIPLE 4:
MASTER YOUR OWN BEHAVIOUR TO INFLUENCE OTHERS

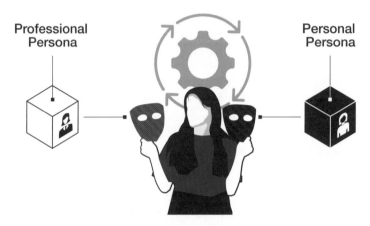

Professional Persona

Personal Persona

Managing behaviour is about managing yourself in order to influence others. The phrase 'classroom management' is almost a misnomer. Teachers are not managing the class; we are managing our own emotions and actions to influence the students in our class. As teachers, we must admit that we have no direct influence over the students in our care. We can't physically move them or force them to be quiet. Instead, we must respect that students are autonomous individuals who are in control of their own thoughts and actions. We can ultimately only master ourselves to influence others.

To begin mastering our own behaviour, we must first identify our own values and beliefs about classroom management. Do you genuinely like working with young people? Do you feel they have value, are inherently good, and deserve your time and patience? In the words of Dylan Wiliam (speaking to a group of graduate teachers):

'I know what you're worried about, you're worried about whether your students will respect you. I have a different worry. I worry about whether you respect your students.'[17]

We must begin with an understanding of our own beliefs because whatever they are, they will come out in our actions.

In managing ourselves, we need to be particularly aware of any sense of frustration or anger when it starts to rise in us. One strategy teachers can use in these situations comes from stoic philosophy. If we are using our behavioural routines and students are not meeting our expectations, there may be a rare occasion that would call for us to raise our voice. If you ever do shout, we encourage you to do it by what the Stoic philosopher Seneca would call 'feigning anger'.[18] If you find yourself shouting in frustration, you've likely waited too long to correct students. Effectively using your tone to communicate the severity of a situation but doing so from a base of relaxation and confidence, rather than frustration, will help you to model the emotional regulation that you are trying to promote in your own students.

It can be hard to master ourselves. Teaching is deeply human work, and it is easy for our professional identity to mix with our private one. Because of this identity mixing, when a student misbehaves, it can be perceived as a personal attack. To circumvent this, it can help to acknowledge the separation between your personal self and your professional self. A disruptive student is not that way because their teacher, 'Josie Smith' (a 20-something cat lover, music fan, sister, wife and friend) told him to sit quietly and finish his work. It's because Josie's professional persona (mathematics teacher) asked him to do some work. When a student rolls his eyes at Josie's request, he isn't rolling them at Josie; he's doing so in response to his maths teacher. Having some professional distance between your personal identity and your teacher role can stop you taking setbacks too personally. This distance helps you to master your own behaviour to ultimately influence others.

17. Dylan Wiliam, Education Research Reading Room Podcast episode #23. 59:07. www.ollielovell.com/dylanwiliam

18. Seneca, L. A. (2019). Anger, mercy, revenge. University of Chicago Press.

PRINCIPLE 5:
BEHAVIOUR IS A CURRICULUM,
TREAT IT AS SUCH

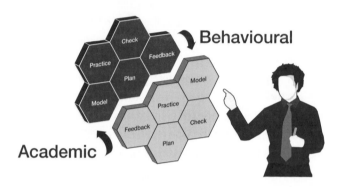

Transfer (the ability to apply ideas learned in one context to a new context) is one of the foundational purposes of all instruction. If we teach students to provide evidence for their arguments in the English classroom, but they never do this in their real lives, our success is severely limited. If we show them how to calculate percentages in maths, but they can't work out how much tax is paid on their first pay check, we have a long way to go.

As Perkins and Grotzer have written, 'transfer is hard to come by, particularly far transfer'.[19] This isn't true just for students, it's true for teachers too. For example, an excellent classroom teacher may seem to forget everything they know about effective instruction when they move from school teaching to adult education and might begin to deliver long and tedious

---

19. Perkins, D. N. and Grotzer, T. A. (1997). Teaching intelligence. American psychologist, 52(10), pg. 1129, as cited in Barnett, S. M. & Ceci, S. J. (2002). When and where do we apply what we learn?: A taxonomy for far transfer. *Psychological Bulletin*, 128(4), pg. 612.

lectures without any checks for understanding. Similarly, a student who may respond appropriately to 'show your thinking' in mathematics may struggle with this skill in humanities.

The point is that any type of teaching, whether it be teaching academic content, or teaching behavioural expectations, is still teaching. Therefore, when we teach students about how to behave effectively in a class, we should ensure that we are transferring all the principles of effective instruction of content to our instruction within the behavioural domain.

Failing to do this, then being surprised when students don't behave well, is the equivalent of a drama teacher putting students on a stage without preparation or rehearsal and then being surprised when they don't know the blocking or their lines. In both cases we're expecting students to act in a certain way, but we aren't giving our students the tools that they need to meet those expectations.

So, let's reflect. What does it take to effectively teach something? A simplified version of Ollie's model of instruction[20] suggests that effective teaching requires the following:

- Plan exactly what you want students to be able to do, say, make, or write
- Introduce the relevance of the content to be taught
- Model it, providing examples and non-examples
- Provide opportunities for student practice
- Check for understanding through both questioning and observation
- Provide feedback and adapt instruction to address knowledge gaps
- Return to the content over time to fight forgetting

These are some of the key steps that effective teachers take when teaching their subject or year level. As it turns out, they're exactly what we need to do when we teach behaviour too! In short, behaviour itself is a curriculum. We must remember teaching behaviour is the same as teaching any other curriculum. We must transfer!

---

20. Lovell, O. (2022). *Tools for Teachers: How to teach, lead, and learn like the world's best educators.* John Catt Educational.

Here are some ideas for how you can follow each of Ollie's seven instructional steps in relation to classroom management:

Component of effective instruction	When applying this idea to the teaching of behaviour...
Plan	Plan exactly how you want students to behave and respond at different parts of the lesson. Don't leave it to chance. Be explicit and specific, not vague and general, e.g. don't just think, 'I want students to enter the class respectfully', think, 'I want students to enter the classroom in a focused way, without talking, to be working on the starter task within 60 seconds, and to have their exercise books open to last lesson's homework for easy checking'.
Relevance	Plan a set of short phrases that simultaneously reinforce expectations, and the reason why they're important, e.g. whilst students are at the door you could introduce your expectations with, 'Remember class, enter silently, commence the starter within 60 seconds, and have your exercise books open to last night's homework *so we can make the most of our learning time today'*.
Model it	Two schools that Ollie has visited, Ted Wragg St Luke's (Exeter, UK) and Challis Community Primary School (Armadale, Australia) model behavioural expectations to students through a collection of videos that capture what it looks like for students to perform the school's routines, and follow its expectations, to a high standard. This is the most powerful way that we've come across of modelling behavioural expectations to students. It equally provides teachers with clear models, which is just as important!
Provide opportunities for practise	Just like all skills, behaviour needs practice (see Principle 2). We wouldn't expect students to complete a multi-step maths problem with 100% accuracy after we've explained it once. In the same way, it's unreasonable for us to expect students to complete a multi-step entry routine (e.g. enter silently, start writing within 60 seconds, exercise books open to last homework) correctly every time and after a single explanation. We can't be afraid to have students rehearse routines. Practice is crucial.
Check for (behavioural) understanding	For students to act in line with expectations, they must be aware of what the expectations are. This means that they must *listen* when those instructions are given. To check whether they have, it can be helpful to simply cold call a student, or multiple students, after you've provided instructions, to check that they've understood. We call this 'checking for behavioural understanding'. Checking for behavioural understanding also occurs through carefully watching as students perform the required behavioural task, noticing gaps between their performance and your expectations, and providing feedback, as outlined in the next box.

Provide feedback and adapt instruction	One of the best and most simple ways to provide feedback for students on behaviour is to scaffold them to self-regulate it. For example, if you want students to enter the classroom within a specific amount of time, display a stopwatch on the screen so that they can monitor how long it takes. Writing up, printing out, and displaying the steps to your regular routines around your classroom is another way to support students to monitor their own behaviour against a clearly communicated standard.
	Once you have these standards clearly in place (which may also include video examples as mentioned under 'Model it'), feedback is as simple as highlighting gaps between students' current behaviour and your expectations, all the while framing opportunities for improvement as a positive rather than as students not meeting the standard. For example, *'That was good, it took us 45 seconds, I'm really excited about us making it excellent! I believe that you can transition from your seats to this mat in under 30 seconds. Let's have another go.'*
	Adapting instruction can also mean responsively scheduling opportunities for students to repeatedly practise core techniques over time, as further outlined in the next box.
Return to the content over time	Just as spaced practice (spreading out practice or retrieval opportunities over time) is helpful in learning academic content, it is also useful in learning behaviour. It is natural for students' memories to decay over time, both for ideas, and for routines. So pre-planned reinforcement is an excellent idea.
	At Dixons Trinity Academy (Bradford, UK), the school has inserted into the timetable specific opportunities for students, and the whole school, to practise key routines and transitions. By pre-scheduling these opportunities, Dixons ensures that all routines are kept to a high standard, and they can also use these time slots responsively depending upon what the school has identified as key focus points.

Teaching is complex, we know how to do it, and how to do it well. When it comes to classroom management, we are empowered by transferring our knowledge from the teaching of content to the teaching of behaviour. Behaviour is a curriculum, treat it as such.

PRINCIPLE 6:
IT'S WHAT YOU SAY AND HOW YOU SAY IT

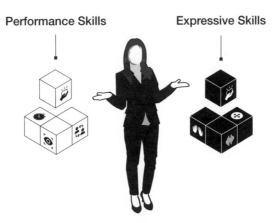

Performance Skills   Expressive Skills

Two teachers can say exactly the same words and get different reactions from students. Why? The difference lies in the way we present and interact with our class. All our non-verbal signals – posture, tone and our facial expressions – impact the effectiveness of our behaviour management practices. To highlight the performance nature of our profession, we draw upon a model from the performing arts. Within this model, performance consists of two key factors: 1. expressive skills and 2. performance skills. Expressive skills include face, voice, movement and gesture.[21] Performance skills include focus, timing, listening, relating and responding to the audience.[22] Let's take a closer look at each of these.

---

21. Melbourne Theatre Company (2022, August 08, Expressive Skills), www.mtc.com.au/discover-more/backstage/expressive-skills/.

22. Ibid.

Expressive skills

Voice: A teacher's voice should vary throughout the lesson. At the start of the lesson, using a loud, clear voice to say 'good morning, eyes this way and listening, thank you' is appropriate. As the class settles, the next direction can be given in a quieter, calmer tone: 'Thank you for settling so quickly.' Instruction can occur in a clear but relaxed voice, and the voice can be suddenly raised for corrections or to gain attention. Modulating our voices helps us to hold students' attention, keep them engaged throughout the lesson, and emphasise as needed.

Language: The more specific we are with our language, the easier it is for our students to understand and follow directions. For example, 'listen up' may be too vague. 'Eyes on me, lips and laptops closed' is a clearer directive. Further, instead of saying 'you may begin', you can describe the behaviours you expect during the task, 'By yourself, and in complete silence, answer question 3'.

Movement and gesture: From the moment students meet a teacher, they are 'sizing them up'. Students immediately want answers to questions like, 'Who is this person?', 'Are they kind or mean?', 'Are they on my team? 'Are they credible?'. We can portray a confident and supportive presence by standing tall, gesturing towards key points during instruction, and acknowledging or correcting students with non-verbal signals. One of the key indicators of a nervous teacher is an unwillingness to cross the imaginary line that lies between the whiteboard and the first row of students' seats. Move into the students' territory to convey your confidence in managing the room.

Performance skills

Focus: Focus is the ability of a performer to remain 'in character'. 'Teacher' is a character we play. One of the questions going through a teacher's mind when in class should be, 'Who does the class need me to be at this point?'. The answer is usually, 'Someone who is calm, consistent and clear'. Staying in this character, especially during times of change, transition, or upheaval within your school is essential for managing a class effectively.

Timing: Teachers need to know *when* to act. An effective teacher knows when to correct a student for calling out (hint: instantly). If a student gets out of a chair, the teacher must judge whether to make an immediate correction, or whether to watch to see if the student moves quietly to the bin to sharpen their pencil, or take some other appropriate action. Timing also includes being reactive, such as knowing when to repeat directions, when to pause for effect during explanations, and how long to give each activity.

Listening, relating, and responding to the audience (class): A great teacher deliberately curates the mood and energy in their class. At times, we need to lift the energy and motivate students to dig deep or focus at the end of a long day. Other times, we need to calm them down, such as before a period of focused independent work or after a busy break. Master teachers can read the energy of the room and use performance skills to manipulate this energy to meet the learning needs of the class.

Underpinning the expressive and performance skills is our 'Way of Being' – the way we relate to our classes. We consider 'warmth' as a general term for demonstrating care towards your students. When we talk to students, we treat them with respect, even when they do the wrong thing. We correct their misbehaviours in a direct and efficient way but understand that we can separate the child from the behaviour. After all, it's helpful to remember that we weren't perfect when we were students ourselves.

This warmth is coupled with a confident sense of calm expectancy. Effective classroom teachers expect students to comply with their requests. This feeling of confidence is often learned through experience and success. For a beginning teacher, allowing 5-8 seconds of take up time after you say 'sitting down, eyes this way and listening' can feel like an eternity. A less effective teacher might begin 'chasing' the class by calling out student names, repeating their requests in a loud and visibly frustrated way. Expecting compliance is conveyed through the performative and expressive skills discussed here. Combining these skills with the tools and routines in the rest of this book will allow you to feel more confident and comfortable in the classroom and for your students to see this too. Remember, students are responding to what you say *and* how you say it.

PRINCIPLE 7:
SUCCESS IS THE GREATEST MOTIVATOR

Many believe that motivation is what leads to success. In reality, this relationship is often the opposite way around, with success being the main factor driving student motivation! Robert Coe, Director of Research and Development at Evidence Based Education, puts it as follows:

> 'Teachers who are confronted with the poor motivation and confidence of low attaining students may interpret this as the cause of their low attainment and assume that it is both necessary and possible to address their motivation before attempting to teach them new material. In fact, the evidence shows that attempts to enhance motivation in this way are unlikely to achieve that end. Even if they do, the impact on subsequent learning is close to zero. In fact, the poor motivation of low attainers is a logical response to repeated failure. **Start getting them to succeed and their motivation and confidence should increase.**'[23]

23. Coe, R., Aloisi, C., Higgins, S. and Major, L. E. (2014). *What makes great teaching? Review of the underpinning research.* p. 23. As cited in Fletcher-Wood, H. (2018). *Responsive teaching: cognitive science and formative assessment in practice.* Routledge.

It's clear. Students behave better when they are experiencing learning success, and the quickest and most efficient way to ensure that success is through clear and explicit instruction. Expert teachers who drive success in this way do at least two things regularly and consistently:[24]

1. Break explanations down into small steps.

2. Use frequent checks for understanding.

Let's dive into each of these a little deeper to help your students have more success in the classroom.

Break skills down into small steps

Working memory can only process a limited amount of information at once.[25] Too much information and we become confused. As a result of this, only after students have mastered the first step, should we introduce the next.

One reason teachers often deliver too much content at once is because of the 'curse of knowledge',[26] a cognitive bias that occurs when a knowledgeable person underestimates the complexity of a task because of how easy they find it themselves. For example, a competent mathematician may be utterly baffled at how a novice can't see that if you need to cook one cup of dry rice for three serves, you need three cups for nine serves (basic proportional reasoning).

As a result of the curse of knowledge, teachers regularly present far too much new information to learners at once. We can attempt to overcome this damaging tendency by purposefully presenting information in small steps and by checking for understanding after each step.

---

24. Rosenshine, B. (2012). Principles of instruction: Research-based strategies that all teachers should know. American educator, 36(1), 12.

25. Lovell, O. (2020). Sweller's Cognitive Load Theory in Action. John Catt Educational.

26. Term originally coined by Robin M. Hogarth, as outlined in Camerer, C., Loewenstein, G. and Weber, M. (1989). The curse of knowledge in economic settings: An experimental analysis. Journal of Political Economy, 97(5), 1232–1254, pg. 1233.

Use frequent checks for understanding

Education experts and authors Tom Sherrington and Doug Lemov both recommend that increasing the number of checks for understanding in a class will improve instruction and achievement. Checking for understanding means getting feedback from students in a way that is quick, efficient, and provides a representative sample of class understanding. This means doing things like using mini whiteboards, asking every student to write, finger voting (often with heads down), picking non-volunteers (cold calling), and utilising hinge questions (questions that determine where to take the lesson next).

The two ideas presented in this chapter – to break skills down into small steps and use frequent checks for understanding – are a taster of what teachers can do to boost student success, and therefore motivation and engagement. But teaching for success is a career-long journey. The main point is to recognise that when students are demotivated, one of the best levers that we can pull is to teach more effectively to ensure greater success.

Success is the greatest motivator. Target your teaching to success and behaviour will often follow.[27]

---

27. See *Tools for Teachers* by Ollie Lovell (www.ollielovell.com/t4t) and *Teach Like a Champion* by Doug Lemov for more on great teaching.

PRINCIPLE 8:
SEEK OUT EXAMPLES OF EXCELLENCE

One of the most powerful things that you can do on your journey to effective behaviour management is to seek out examples of excellence. Through books like this one, we can gain insights and advice into *what* teachers do to promote classroom management. However, what we *cannot* get from these forms of media is a clear understanding of just how high 'high standards' can get.

That's why I (Ollie) organised a trip to England to see some of that country's highest performing schools in action (most notably Michaela Community School, Dixons Trinity Academy, and Reach Academy Feltham). What I saw absolutely blew me away. The tightness of the routines, the focus of the students, the academic rigour, the standards, and expectations of the teachers were all beyond what I thought was possible!

When I visited these schools, I knew lots of theories about classroom management. I knew the steps that I needed to take, but I didn't truly understand just how focused students could be until I saw it with my own eyes. It was a transformative experience and I returned home with a renewed belief about how focused classrooms could be. Young people were capable of more than I ever expected, I just needed to see it to believe it.

This effect also occurs locally. I recently coached a first year teacher who, during deliberate practice, was able to do all the right things to set up a highly effective entry routine. His tone was right, his phrasing, positioning, everything was great, except the outcome.

For some reason, he was struggling to translate this to his lessons. After three coaching rounds on the same action step,[28] we managed to identify what was holding him back. He hadn't seen enough successful examples of a focused entry. The standard that he was holding his students to wasn't high enough because he hadn't seen how quietly and efficiently students could enter the classroom. To try to address this, we arranged a visit to another class for him to see the same routine in action.

After the visit, this was his reaction (taken from a video recording of our debrief):

[The visit] was helpful because I saw the way that you actually reinforced the same standards with your group. But it also let me see the way that students responded to it. Because sometimes, even subconsciously, you're like, 'Oh, are they really going to do this? Are they going to go out [of the classroom] and do it [re-enter the classroom properly] again when I ask them to?' But actually seeing the positive impact it had was encouraging and showed me that if I keep working on getting this right, this is the benefit [a silent and highly focused start to the lesson] that I can end up with.

---

28. See www.steplab.co to explore instructional coaching action steps and to learn more about evidence informed Instructional Coaching.

It isn't just teachers who are limited by what they have seen in terms of classroom behaviour, it's also students. Often students have only seen poor behaviour and are limited by their own beliefs about how well they can listen, how responsive they can be, and how much they can learn in a lesson. This can be addressed in a number of ways, but one particularly effective strategy is to work to establish really high standards in one of the classes in your school (e.g. all students working silently within 60 seconds of entering the room), then put together a collection of video recordings that capture this standard that can then be shared throughout the school (this was also discussed in Principle 5: Behaviour is a curriculum, treat it as such).

In the words of the American civil and children's rights activist, Marian Wright Edelman, 'You can't be what you can't see'. Seek out examples of excellence to change what you and others believe is possible. 'High standards' are probably much higher than you think!

PRINCIPLE 9:
STUDENTS NEED TO KNOW THEY BELONG
AND THAT YOU BELIEVE IN THEM

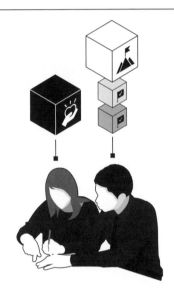

It is common to have misconceptions about student behaviour. When I (Ollie) began teaching, I held a fundamental misconception. I'm ashamed to say it, but that misconception was: 'When you tell a student off, they need to leave that conversation knowing that you're disappointed in them.' I don't exactly know where I got this idea, but I do know the effect. It resulted in me finishing potentially restorative conversations with flat and demotivating lines like, *'Do better next time'* and *'It's not good enough.'*

The effect? Those students who lagged became more demotivated and fell further behind. I saw and felt this effect, but I honestly didn't know what I was doing wrong. It wasn't until I spoke to Tom Bennett on the ERRR podcast,[29] and he said the following, that I realised my error:

'...when you finish the detention... a student needs to feel like, "They want me in the class, they want me to do better, I can do better, and know how to do better".'

When Tom said this, it hit me like a ton of bricks. I'd been doing it wrong all this time. No wonder my disengaged students were getting *more* disengaged, I was *making* them more disengaged by instilling a sense of shame about their performance. Even worse, I wasn't giving them any indication that I believed that they *could* do the right thing. [See Routine 6 for a practical script on how to have such a positive-ending conversation with a student.]

The need to belong is one of our strongest motivators.[30] As educators, it falls upon us to assist our students in fulfilling this need. But how can we do it? How do we simultaneously correct our students while showing that we believe in them and that they belong? There are three strategies you can use to achieve this: Avoid deficit theorising, find common ground, and witness the good.

Finding common ground and witnessing the good will be dealt with under Principle 10: Bank positivity. Thus, below we describe the idea of deficit theorising and why it must be avoided in your class.

Deficit theorising: This idea, which we first came across through the work of Professor Russell Bishop,[31] asserts that one of the most dangerous things that we can do as leaders of young people is to start with limiting assumptions about what they can achieve. These limiting assumptions often stem from our own beliefs about their socioeconomic or cultural backgrounds, or knowledge of their past achievement. The problem

29. www.ollielovell.com/tombennett

30. Baumeister, R. F. and Leary, M. R. (2017). The need to belong: Desire for interpersonal attachments as a fundamental human motivation. *Interpersonal development*, 57–89.

31. www.ollielovell.com/errr/russellbishop/

with such limiting beliefs is that they don't stay locked up inside us, they come out, they impact how we treat students, and they impact student achievement.[32]

If we believe that a student can't understand complex concepts, we won't take as much time to explain an idea with them as we might another student. If we don't believe they can manage their time, we won't be as patient in supporting them to write their homework in their diary or set implementation intentions and action triggers.[33] And if we don't believe that students can behave to a high standard, we're less likely to take the crucial steps that will lead to their behaviour improving.

In Principle 6: It's what you say and how you say it, we talked about the importance of 'calm expectancy' – talking in a tone that gives students the feeling that it is inevitable that they will do what you're requesting and can achieve the high standards you set. Deficit theorising is the opposite. It is acting from a core belief that the students you're working with can't make the grade.

For students to strive, for students to feel like they belong, and for students to improve and achieve, they need to know that you believe in them.

---

32. Friedrich, A., Flunger, B., Nagengast, B., Jonkmann, K. and Trautwein, U. (2015). Pygmalion effects in the classroom: Teacher expectancy effects on students' math achievement. *Contemporary Educational Psychology, 41*, 1–12.

33. www.ollielovell.com/olliesclassroom/implementation-intentions-action-triggers/

PRINCIPLE 10:
BANK POSITIVITY

In working with students as a house coordinator or year level leader, you often come across students who say things like, 'That teacher hates me'. A student who feels this way is very unlikely to want to behave in that teacher's classroom. Now, of course the teacher doesn't hate the student, but when you visit the class, you may find that almost every interaction between the teacher and student is negative or corrective. It's '*stop talking*' or '*get back to work*', etc. Any positivity is vastly outweighed by the teacher telling the student that they aren't doing well enough, it's easy to see why the student might feel that the teacher hates them. The cure for this is to build positive relationships with each and every student.

Positive relationships are built through positive interactions, and banking positivity is all about deliberately curating these interactions. Two specific approaches to banking positivity first mentioned in Principle 9 are **finding common ground** with your students and **witnessing the good**. It's important to do this early and with purpose. Finding common ground means you deliberately look for interests or life experiences you have in common. Witnessing the good can mean highlighting positive personality traits or a specific effort that a student made. These two actions help to build a stronger relationship with each student and, the stronger the relationship, the more you can challenge their behaviour and push them to be successful.

The crucial work of **finding common ground**[34] can begin even before the new school year has started. If you know that you're going to have some potentially disruptive students in your class next year, see if you can catch them in the yard or in the hall and have one-to-one conversations. Try to find out what they're interested in. Do you share an interest? If so, you can build on that to have positive conversations. If you don't share an interest, that's okay, simply asking the student about their interests is often enough to begin to build the relationship.

If the new year has already started, it still isn't too late to find common ground. It's often valuable to have conversations before class when students are outside the room or at the end of class when packing up. This has the benefit of building relationships while keeping the time during class focused on teaching and learning content. Regardless of when or how it's done, finding common ground will go a long way to bolstering positive behaviour in your classes.

Once they are in your class, do your best to **witness the good**.[35] Knowing that students may struggle to conform to classroom expectations some time down the track, do your best to provide affirmation of any good work or behaviour they demonstrate in the first few lessons. It can be particularly valuable to send a message home to parents highlighting something positive they've done.

34. Knight, J. (2015). *Better Conversations: Coaching Ourselves and Each Other To Be More Credible, Caring, and Connected.* Corwin Press.

35. Knight, J. (2012). *High-Impact Instruction: A Framework for Great Teaching.* Corwin Press.

Further, teachers can witness the good through the teaching tool 'positive narration'. For example, when students are transitioning from one task to another (such as from the starter to the instructional phase of the lesson) the teacher highlights students who are on track, e.g., *'Simon has already written the learning intention for the day. Sophie is ruling her margin. Shuqi is carefully writing the date'*, etc. This acknowledges the students who are on track, as well as highlighting the norm of a quick and efficient transition, to the whole class.

The key benefit of witnessing the good through positive narration and other techniques is that we shift the ratio of affirming vs. corrective interactions in our classroom. Without deliberately employing these techniques, a teacher will likely find themselves giving three to four corrections for every affirmation in the classroom. When we purposefully bank positivity, we can positively flip that ratio so that students are hearing far more affirmations than corrections.

You can bank positivity with parents too. If a student behaves well in the first three classes, we recommend contacting home with a simple email, *'Dear (parents names). Just a quick message to let you know that (student name) has made a great start in science. She has been polite, organised and focused in class. I'm looking forward to working with her more this year.'* Getting on the front foot in this way means that if corrective contact does need to be made later on, it's made from a stronger foundation.

Bank positivity by finding common ground and witnessing the good. It often only takes one conversation to create a little shift in a student's attitude and to increase your chances of having a positive and productive relationship. As humans, we all crave positive relationships with others. As teachers, it's our role to take the lead and create them.

PART 2: SCRIPTS

What to expect in Part 2

Part 2 of this book is designed to give you concrete advice on how to run your class in a calm and focused way, and in line with the ten principles of classroom management outlined in part 1. Many classroom management books stop at general advice. Others get as far as tips. But very rarely do guides give you explicit guidance regarding exactly what you can say and do to be successful in achieving a calm and productive classroom. This is the goal in part 2.

Why scripts?

As we stated in Principle 2: The best classroom managers have the best habits:

> *Expert teachers have automated effective routines for each part of the lesson; entry routine, settling the class, monitoring independent work, reacting to disruptions, responding to common misconceptions. Mastering and automatising these basics frees up students' minds to be more adaptable, responsive, and effective in new and complex situations.*

All teachers will have automated routines, but it's only expert teachers who have automated *effective* routines. The way to develop these effective, automated routines is to purposefully build them. Scripting your words and your actions, in detail, is the first step to doing this. Most teachers' behaviour becomes automatic around the time that teacher effectiveness begins to level off.[36] So it's better to script these words early in a career to ensure that the habits that you're building are effective ones.

Some people argue against the use of scripts, suggesting that they undermine teachers' autonomy by telling them what to say. However, arguing against scripts is fundamentally an argument against worked examples. Such an argument runs counter to a mountain of evidence from the cognitive sciences which clearly demonstrates that worked examples are incredibly effective at building the expertise of novices.[37]

It's a mistake to think that providing a student with a worked example for the correct use of commas will somehow restrict their use of commas to only that specific context in future. Similarly, it's a mistake to believe that providing scripts to teachers will somehow limit their responses to students in future.

Ultimately, we agree with Doug Lemov's assertion that to assume scripts limit teachers is a gross underestimation of teachers. Instead, it's the case that, '[teachers] *because they are smart and independent minded, begin to adapt and internalise almost immediately, making any routine their own.*'[38] A scripted routine is a crucial scaffold to support great teaching and we invite you to use the scripts herein as a springboard for your own expertise. Modify them, adapt them, and make them your own; rehearse them to build the habits of an expert!

---

36. Hobbiss, M., Sims, S. and Allen, R. (2021). Habit formation limits growth in teacher effectiveness: A review of converging evidence from neuroscience and social science. *Review of Education*, 9(1), 3–23.

37. Sweller, J. (2006). The worked example effect and human cognition. *Learning and instruction.*

38. Lemov et. al., (2022) *Reconnect, Building School Culture for Meaning, Purpose and Belonging*

TOOLS, ROUTINES AND SCRIPTS

There are three building blocks that form the basis of part 2 of this book – tools, routines, and scripts – and it's important for us to provide clarity as to the differences between the three.

Tools are the individual techniques that will form the foundation of your behaviour management strategy. The table below defines the ten of the most essential tools for teachers to master. The full list can be found in the glossary.

Tool	Definition and example
Check for behavioural understanding	Ask a student (or students) to repeat your expectations to check they've understood: *'Can you repeat back to me the three things we need to do when we enter the classroom?'*
Describe and direct	If a student is off-task, describe their behaviour and direct them to the desired behaviour: *'You are out of your seat, sit down and focus on your work thanks'.*
Directed choice[39]	Give students a choice about their behaviour: *'You can be quiet and focus on your work or you can move to another seat in the room, your choice.'*
Make expectations explicit	Be clear when making statements to students. *'Listen up'* is not clear. *'Eyes on me, no talking, listening to the instructions'* is more specific.
Non-verbal	Use hand signals to silently direct behaviour e.g. *finger to lips* for shh, *palms open* for open books.
Positive narration[40]	Describe, in a clear voice, instances of positive behaviour in the class to reinforce the expected norm: *'The front row have started working silently'.*
Prime	Give students an indication of what is about to happen: *'You have one minute to finish the activity, then wait silently with eyes on me'.*

---

39. Rogers, B. (1997). *Cracking The Hard Class*. Sage Publications.

40. Lemov, D. (2010). *Teach Like A Champion: 49 techniques that put students on the path to college (K-12)*. John Wiley & Sons.

Timer	Use an easily visible timer to clarify how long students have to complete an activity: *'This task will take us 15 minutes. As soon as the timer begins, you can start working silently, thanks.'*
W. I. N. conversation[41]	A structured conversation when you keep students after class consisting of three key points: *1. What happened? 2. What was the Impact? 3. Next steps to make this right...*
100%[42]	Make sure all students are paying complying with the request. Not most students, every last one.

Many of the tools within this book come from the work of others (e.g. Doug Lemov, Bill Rogers), but many are also original.

Routines are created by stringing together several tools to achieve a broader goal. One broader goal could be 'Students enter the class calmly and quietly and begin learning promptly', which we could give the title 'entry routine'. A collection of tools that could be strung together to achieve this end could be:

Scripts are detailed plans of the exact words and actions that a teacher will use to carry out a routine. They're a concrete plan that is well thought out and rehearsed. These routines aid a teacher in reaching their goal as quickly and efficiently as possible.

By combining tools into routines and planning routines with scripts, you should be able to swiftly generate positive behavioural change in your classroom.

Summary

- Tools are the individual techniques that will form the foundation of your behaviour management strategy.

- Routines are created by stringing together several tools to achieve a broader goal.

---

41. The W.I.N. model was developed by the team at Brighton Grammar School, Melbourne.

42. Lemov, D. (2010). *Teach like a champion: 49 techniques that put students on the path to college (K-12).* John Wiley & Sons.

- Scripts are detailed plans of the exact words and actions that a teacher will use to carry out a routine.

Within this book, tools, routines and scripts are all combined into a quick-reference table format, as follows:

Routine name		
Tool	Teacher talk and action	Notes
Tool name	*Teacher script in italics.* Teacher actions, or options for teacher actions, will be in non-italicised script here.	You will find additional notes here that will help you know how or when to implement this tool.

What about when...?

Within part 2, you will also see a section entitled 'What about when...?' following most of the routines. These are additional routines and steps that teachers can take if the routine doesn't lead to the expected outcome. They address specific situations that often arise and common challenges that teachers often face when attempting to establish more positive and productive behavioural norms. We hope that you find these 'What about when...?' sections a useful supplement to the main scripts.

Remember to rehearse!

There's one point that we can't stress enough as you embark upon the scripts that follow. That is to remember to rehearse! We emphasised this idea in the title of Principle 2: The best classroom managers have the best habits... and habits are created through deliberate practice.

For each of the following routines and scripts, study it, adapt it to make it your own, then *rehearse* it! You can do this rehearsal with anyone and in any context. *However*, rehearsal will have more impact the more realistic it is and the better matched it is to the context in which the technique is to be used. One great idea is to have a few friendly colleagues act as students and support you to rehearse in the exact classroom you're going to enact the routine. They should play the roles of students whom you're likely to need to use the routines on!

Good luck and make sure you remember to rehearse.

SOME ROUTINES FOR THE FIRST LESSON WITH A NEW CLASS

Your first lesson with a new class is a crucial time to establish yourself as the fair, knowledgeable authority within the classroom, and to make your expectations clear for the year to come. There are two key things that are valuable to do in a first lesson that differ from what you would usually do in a standard class: 1. A subject and teacher introduction and 2. Sharing of the class expectations.

Subject and teacher introduction

You can, and should, plan and practise exactly what you are going to say to introduce yourself and the subject to students in your first lesson. This maximises the probability of your message coming across exactly as you want it to. There are many goals you may have for your subject and teacher introduction but, in most cases, you will want to do the following. You will want to communicate to students that:

1. You (the students) can be successful this year if you put in the effort.

2. I (the teacher) care about you and am committed to helping you to achieve that success.

3. I (the teacher) am competent and fair.

In addition (and especially if you're new to a school), it can be useful to ask experienced colleagues questions like, 'What do students really care about at this school?' or 'What are some of the main fears or worries that these students may have when coming into a new year?' This empowers you to adapt your first lesson script to address any other particularly pertinent points.

Here are two examples of such an introductory script.

Ollie addresses a Year 12 mathematics class

Good morning, everybody. I'm Mr Lovell and this year I'll be taking you for further mathematics.

I really like teaching further maths because it's a subject in which any student can be successful if they're willing to put in the work. Being successful in further mathematics is a matter of being diligent, organised, and working hard. And it's my goal to assist you in doing that this year (Point 1 from pg. 52).

My number one goal is to help you to achieve your target study score in your final exams, and I will do everything in my power to help you to achieve that (Point 2).

If you're wondering about me at all, I'm in my x^{th} year of teaching this subject and I've also worked as an [examination board] assessor for it, so I know exactly what the examiners are looking for. Throughout the year I'll be giving you clear and specific advice about what you need to be effective in this class, and I'll require you to follow that advice carefully and precisely to maximise your chances of success (Point 3).

That's a little about me. Here's what I need from you this year. [On to class expectations]

Mark addresses a Year 8 physical education class

Good morning, I'm Dr. Dowley and this year I'll be taking you for Year 8 physical education.

I love teaching PE because it's important for our health and wellbeing. Taking care of our bodies and our minds is an essential part of life and PE teaches you how to do that.

Importantly, it doesn't matter if you've played sport your whole life or maybe you haven't been interested in sport so far. That's okay, this course isn't about how skillful you are, it's an opportunity to try new things and get moving. All you need to do to succeed is to listen, be organised and have a go. All we are aiming to do is to share some new skills with you, keep you active and take you from where you are now to a slightly healthier and more knowledgeable version of yourself. (Point 1)

My aim for the first few weeks is for us to respect each other. I'll aim to earn your respect by being organised, consistent and fair. You can show respect by listening when I'm speaking and being kind to each other. (Point 2)

I've played lots of sports over my time, cricket, football, basketball, triathlons, tennis, I was also a gym instructor and athletics coach. I love this stuff and I'm excited to share some of the things I've learned with you. (Point 3)

To begin, here are some expectations that we have, which will ensure we have a great year together...

Sharing class expectations

A well-managed class, and school, will have several foundational principles or values upon which it is run. These will be referred to frequently by the teacher, as well as acting as reference points for restorative conversations with students (see Routine 6). A first lesson is a great opportunity to begin to introduce these foundation principles and you should plan to deepen students' exposure to and understanding of these principles each lesson for the first few weeks.

A good set of class expectations will be concise (aim for three key ideas), clear (language should be student friendly and unambiguous) and framed in positive language ('be kind' rather than 'no put downs'). Here are some examples of possible class expectations:

Example 1: Prepared, polite, productive:[43]

In this classroom, students are...		
Prepared	**Polite**	**Productive**
This means:	This means:	This means:
■ Arrive to class on time	■ Use people's names	■ Follow teacher instructions and stay on-task
■ Bring:	■ No: 'I agree with what he said'	■ Take actions to support rather than disrupt your own and your classmates' learning
■ Calculator	■ Yes: 'I agree with what Bilal said'	
■ Workbook		
■ Textbook	■ No: 'Hey sir' or 'Hey mister'	■ Helpful: Quick and efficient transitions
■ Pencil	■ Yes: 'Excuse me Mr Lovell'	
■ Eraser	■ Professional written correspondence	■ Disruptive: Calling out, delaying class progress
■ Ruler		
■ Completed homework	■ E.g., start emails with 'I hope you're having a good day' or 'I trust your weekend was restful'	■ Be proactive and assertive when it comes to your learning
■ To signal your readiness to learn:		■ Do: Ask for help when you need it
■ Enter quietly	■ Express gratitude and appreciation for teachers' and classmates' efforts	■ Do: Provide (polite) feedback to the teacher
■ Take off your hat		
■ Be on the lookout for the first learning task	■ Be kind to each other	

Notice that these expectations are short, sweet and memorable (alliteration: prepared, polite, productive) and they're accompanied by specific examples and non-examples of appropriate behaviour.

Also of note is that there's quite a lot in the above and introducing it all in one go is likely to overwhelm students. Instead, it can work well to introduce your three-part framework over a few lessons. You could briefly introduce the 'Three P' framework in the first lesson, then provide detail and examples about points 1, 2, and 3 across the next three lessons.

---

43. This example is taken from *Tools for Teachers: How to teach, lead, and learn like the world's best educators*, (Lovell, 2022).

Example 2: Respect, integrity, learning, accountability:[44]

Another good approach is to base your expectations on your school's values and make it explicit to students how these translate to classroom behaviour and engagement. The table below outlines what a behaviour expectations poster could look like for a school where the school values are respect, integrity, learning and accountability

In this classroom, students demonstrate	
Respect	**Integrity**
This means:	This means:
■ Use people's names	■ Be honest and clear when it comes to your learning
■ Don't say: 'I agree with what he said.'	■ Do: Show integrity when you don't understand by asking for help
■ Do say: 'I agree with what Bilal said.'	■ Do: Provide (polite) feedback to the teacher when you see opportunities for improvement
■ Don't say: 'Hey sir' or 'Hey mister.'	
■ Do say: 'Excuse me, Mr Lovell.'	
■ Professional written correspondence	
■ E.g. Start emails with, 'Dear Dr Dowley, I hope you're having a good day' or 'Dear Dr Dowley, I trust your weekend was restful'	
■ Express gratitude and appreciation for teachers' and classmates' efforts	
■ Be kind to each other	
Learning	**Accountability**
This means:	This means:
■ To signal your enthusiasm and readiness to learn	■ Arrive to class on time
■ Enter quietly	■ Bring
■ Take off your hat	■ Calculator
■ Be on the lookout for the first learning task	■ Workbook
■ Take actions to support a positive and enthusiastic learning environment in the classroom	■ Textbook
■ Be helpful: Quick and efficient transitions	■ Pencil
■ Don't be disruptive: Calling out, delaying class progress	■ Eraser
	■ Ruler
	■ Completed homework
	■ Follow teacher instructions and stay on-task

As can be seen, the actual expectations (concrete examples) are almost identical in both example 1 and example 2. This is because the concrete

---

44. Adapted from Brighton Grammar's four values of respect, integrity, passion, and accountability.

actions that we want students to follow are usually pretty consistent, and this gives us flexibility to communicate these expectations to students through a variety of formats or frameworks.

It's often most effective to build on and strengthen an existing framework (such as the school's values) rather than introduce new terminology in your own individual classroom. Consistency of messaging also makes it easier for the students to remember, so they don't need to learn a new set of expectations for each teacher. If there doesn't seem appetite at the school leadership level to establish a unified approach to class expectations, small groups can band together to construct and reinforce them too (at the same time as reconsidering their choice of school!).

In summary, an effective first lesson with a new class can look like:

1. An entry routine;

2. subject and teacher introduction;

3. introducing class expectations;

4. begin teaching and learning!

In your first lesson it can also be useful to conduct some activities or surveys with students to get to know them and show your interest in them. For more on some of these options, see chapter 2 of Ollie's book *Tools for Teachers*.

ROUTINE 1: ENTRY ROUTINE

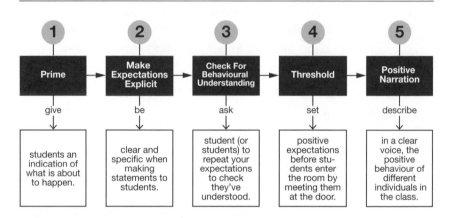

An entry routine captures the way in which we want students to enter the classroom and begin their first task. Establishing an entry routine ensures that students start learning and working from the minute that they enter the classroom. It shows to them that we value the learning time we have together and that it's important that we use this time well. A focused start sets the tone for the rest of the lesson. Entry routines also serve as a fantastic opportunity for routine rehearsal with your class, and a great early win with classroom management.

The routine

Entry routine		
Tool	*Teacher talk* **and action**	**Notes**
1. Prime	*Good morning, eyes on me, no talking thanks* [wait for attention], *thank you. I'm looking forward to seeing a focused and productive entry to make the most of our learning time today.*	Delivered at the door, before students enter the class. This sentence tunes students in and lets them know what is coming next.
2. Make expectations explicit	*There are three expectations: 1. Enter silently, 2. Sit in your assigned seat, 3. Begin the starter activity in under 60 seconds.*	Hold up three fingers to indicate the three requirements. Adapt to your context. For example, substitute 'silently' for 'calmly' or another descriptive word or phrase of your choice.
3. Check for behavioural understanding	*What's the first expectation* [pause], *Harry?* *What's the second expectation* [pause], *Amal?* And so on.	Important: Questions come before names to ensure that all students are listening. Repeat as required if students are struggling to recall the routine.
4. Threshold	*Enter silently, thank you.*	Stand at the doorway in a position such that you can see inside and outside the room simultaneously. Use a quiet voice to greet students by name on their way in. Use your arm like a 'boom gate' to control the flow of students and ensure they enter one at a time if necessary.
5. Positive narration	*Harry is silent, thank you. Frances has begun the starter. Tracey is already on question 2…* etc.	You can also accentuate positive narration with the names of five or so 'fast starters' written on the board.

What about when…?

#WAW: Students' don't follow the entry routine		
Tool	*Teacher talk* and action	Notes
Do it again (individual)	*Harry, you forgot the 'silent' part, let's try that again. Please head out and practise coming in silently. You've got this. Thanks.*	This is the first opportunity for students to see that you mean what you say. Be prepared and primed to uphold your standards whilst establishing the entry routine. If you don't, behaviour can begin to slip very quickly. End with 'thanks', not 'please', to communicate your implicit expectation that the student will comply with your request.
Or do it again (whole class)	*Eyes and ears this way thanks. We had three expectations on entering: 1. Enter silently, 2. Begin the starter right away, 3. All pens writing within 60 seconds. With a hand up, I'd like someone to tell me which one of these we forgot,* [student response]. *That's right, Tibian, we forgot to enter silently, so we now have a chance to practise that again. Leave your books, but let's move calmly and respectfully out of the classroom now to give it another go. Thank you.*	Deliver with a positive, enthusiastic tone… Be enthusiastic to give students an opportunity to practise and improve their entry routine. You could even add a phrase like, '*Every improvement we make now will help us to have more learning time each lesson for the rest of the year!*' to reinforce the 'why' of refining entry routines.

#WAW: Students consistently struggling to settle into work		
Tool	*Teacher talk* and action	**Notes**
Seating plan	Script to introduce seating plan: *Starting class in a focused way is absolutely key because it ensures that we make the most of our valuable learning time. To help us with this, we have a seating plan. You can see it on the board. When you enter class today, ensure that you take your assigned seat.* [Continue with the usual entry routine from pg. 59.] If a student asks, *Will we have this seating plan every lesson?* Reply with, *Our focus at the moment is a strong start John, I want you 100% focused on that. Thank you.* You could also add, *If you think the seating plan isn't conducive to your learning, you can come and see me after class to discuss further. Thanks.*	A well-constructed seating plan helps you learn the names of your students, provide opportunities for peer learning and minimises disruptions. We recommend them for students of all ages. Display the seating plan on the board at the start of each lesson until students are used to it. The seating plan should be from students' perspective with the front of class/teacher's desk at top of screen. You may like to have a second version of the seating plan from your own perspective (front of class at the bottom of the page) on your desk. This also helps you learn names quickly and to make brief notes on student work, attention, or behaviour. If you don't know the students in your class well as yet, you can ask other teachers to review your seating plan prior to implementation to see if they have any suggested improvements. Don't be afraid to change a seating plan if it isn't working. Showing the students that you're willing to swiftly respond to student behaviour reinforces that you are committed to a calm and focused classroom to support their learning.

#WAW: Students are late		
Tool	*Teacher talk* and action	Notes
Make expectations explicit (regarding how to enter in a respectful way when late)	*If you are late, arrive at the door and wait quietly. I'll wave you in and you come in silently. Take your seat as quickly as possible and copy what everyone else is doing.* Give non-example: *Don't slam the door, shout out 'sorry miss, I had to get a drink' then bang your books down. You are late, sneak in like a burglar. When I'm done instructing, I'll come speak to you.*	Distilling this script down into two or three key points that suit your classroom context (e.g. when you come in late, wait for a wave then sneak in silently) will make it more memorable for students.

ROUTINE 2: DEFUSE DEBATE

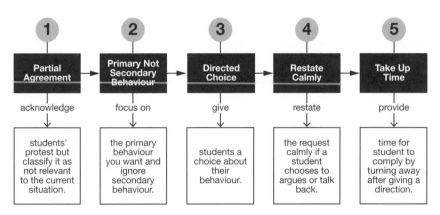

One of the primary patterns of interaction that undermines effective classroom management is the student–teacher debate. You've likely experienced this yourself. Perhaps you've made a simple request like:

> *'Please put your headphones away'*, and had a student reply with something like,

> *'But Mr. Jones lets me listen to music in class!'*

You rebut, *'Put them away thanks, they are a distraction'*.

To which the student replies, *'No, they help me concentrate'*.

'They are a distraction and if I let you use them then other people will think it's ok as well.'

'But that isn't fair because…'

…and the debate goes on!

Even if students do have a valid reason to debate a ruling that you've made in the classroom, the time and place for that discussion is not whilst you're trying to teach the rest of the class, or during a time when students should be focused on independent practice. Expert teachers expect and plan for these scenarios. The role of the teacher in this situation is to defuse the debate, uphold the standards, and refocus the student on learning.

Defuse debate		
Tool	*Teacher talk* and action	Notes
1. Partial agreement[45]	Teacher: *Neha, I know you don't mean to, but you're talking a bit loudly. Quietly focus on your work, thanks.* Student: *Other students are talking too …* Teacher: *Maybe so* (partial agreement)*, but we're talking about you and your work, back to it, thanks.*	Expect a counter response from students and respond in a way that doesn't escalate the discussion. Other partial agreement phrases (in addition to 'Maybe so') include, 'Even so', 'Even if', 'That may be true' and 'That may be the case'. Avoid saying *'I don't care what other students are doing'*. It is a negative and ineffective response.
2. Primary, not secondary behaviour	[Teacher doesn't react]	A student may roll their eyes, mutter under their breath, or move in an exaggerated way whilst they comply with your request. Avoid saying *'Don't you roll your eyes at me'.* Tactically ignore these secondary behaviours and focus on the primary behaviour, which is whether or not the student is acting in line with your request. You can address the secondary behaviours at the end of class as required.

---

45. Rogers, B. (2011). *You know the fair rule: strategies for positive and effective behaviour management and discipline in schools.* Australian Council for Education Research.

3. Directed choice[46]	*Neha, your voice is still too loud and disrupting the class. You can choose to either stop talking now or you can be moved to another seat where you can better make the most of your learning time. The choice is yours.*	Clearly link the student behaviour (talking loudly) to the outcome (disrupting the class) and show that they have a choice in what happens.
4. Restate calmly	Teacher: *'Neha, you chose to keep talking. Move to this seat at the front so you can get some work done, thank you.'* Student: *'No, I'll be good now, give me one more chance'* Teacher: *'Move to the front of the room thanks Neha.'* Student: *'It wasn't even me, someone else was doing it'* Teacher (with hand out in front to say, stop): *'Neha, this isn't a debate. Move to the front of the room, thank you.'*	Expect to repeat instructions. Do so with a calm, but firm voice. Your body language should signal that you expect the student to comply. Avoid showing any frustration The phrase 'This isn't a debate' is one of the most useful phrases in the teacher's *defuse debate* toolkit.
5. Take up time	*I'll be back in 30 seconds and I expect you to be sitting in that chair* [points to front row chair]. *Thank you.*	Don't stand over a student waiting for them to comply. This creates a power battle. Instead, give them 'take up time' so they can save some face by having a small amount of choice by moving in their own time (as long as it's within the specified time limit). Then turn away and attend to another student before checking back in in 30 seconds (or whichever time limit you specify) End with 'thank you', not 'please', to communicate your implicit expectation that they will comply with your request.

---

46. Ibid.

What about when...?

#WAW Student asks 'This is boring, when am I ever going to use this?'		
Tool	*Teacher talk* and action	Notes
Partial agreement	Student: *This is so boring.* Teacher: *Maybe it is, but it's the work we are doing now. Do you need my help to get started?* Student: *When am I ever going to use this?* Teacher: *I can't predict the future but it's the work we are doing now. Or: You'll need this knowledge for next year, back to it thanks.*	Students often make this comment when they don't understand the work. Rather than give an elaborate explanation for the why, aim to redirect and help them to be successful in learning it. See Principle 7: Success is the greatest motivator.

#WAW A student flat out refuses to comply		
Tool	*Teacher talk* and action	Notes
Directed choice	*Neha, I can't force you to do anything. But I have asked you to move, and you seem to have chosen not to for now. However, It's important for me to let you know that making that choice means that I'll have to follow up with the head of house/year level coordinator later and it will also mean a phone call to your parents. You have 30 seconds to decide, I encourage you to be sitting in your new seat within those 30 seconds for a focused second half of the lesson. You were focused last lesson, I know you can show me that again.*	Refusing a reasonable request needs to be escalated. Remain calm, be clear about the consequences, and give plenty of take up time. Ensure you finish with an encouraging and restorative comment.

A student says 'what did I do wrong'		
Tool	*Teacher talk* and action	Notes
Primary, not secondary behaviour	Student: *What did I do wrong?* Teacher: *I've been clear about your behaviour Neha. Now, we have 10 minutes left of class. Let's not dwell on what's happened but instead focus on making the most of these final 10 minutes. That means sitting silently and working on the draft of your essay. Let's have a look at where you're up to…*	If you don't want to describe the negative behaviour to the student (or if you didn't see it yourself). Saying 'you know what you did' allows you to move on to the more productive 'next steps' phase of the conversation. For follow up, see Routine 6: After Class Conversation.

ROUTINE 3: TEACHER SELF-REGULATION

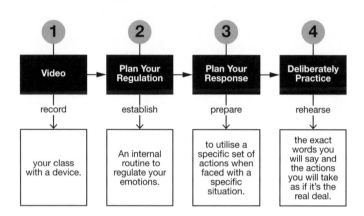

A major challenge in behaviour management is managing ourselves. At times, we can feel frustrated, angry, triggered, upset, or on edge when we have a series of lessons in which student behaviour is getting in the way of learning. These negative feelings can then act as barriers to us managing the classroom effectively because, as was emphasised in Principle 4, we must master our own behaviour, and be positive role models, in order to be able to influence others. It's therefore valuable to have steps and processes to proactively and reactively regulate ourselves in the classroom. The following steps are useful if you periodically feel like your head is going to explode during lessons with a particular class (or even with multiple classes!).

The routine

Note: The tools provided in the table need not be used in sequence. Rather, they are more of a set of options for you to choose from depending upon your context and preferences.

Teacher self-regulation		
Tool	*Teacher talk* and action	Notes
Video	[Video record your class]	Recording your class is extremely helpful because it helps you to view the lesson, students' behaviours, and your reactions, at a time when you're in a more relaxed state.
		Doing this can help you to see the chain of events leading up to a student's behaviour. This includes how poor behaviour is set off and who initiates it, how you react, and what the follow-on results are.
		Put simply, a video helps you to clearly diagnose what is occurring in your classroom. Often when a teacher views a video of their class, they realise that it isn't a case of all students acting up all the time, but rather a few key students who are being disruptive at a few key times, and often in predictable ways. This clarity provides a solid basis for feeling more relaxed about 'that challenging class' (as you often realise it's only a few disruptive students), and places you well to strategically plan your response.
Plan your regulation	Some options: - Stand tall - Deep breath - Smile - Repeat a positive mantra to yourself, e.g. *This learning experience will help me to become an effective classroom manager.* - Look at each student one-by-one and say to yourself, 'on-task' or 'off-task' to get a clearer picture of the true level of class engagement.	These options listed left can be combined into a routine that you can run through to centre yourself when it feels like the class is getting out of control. You must ground yourself before you can ground the class. (See Principle 4: Master your own behaviour to influence others.) I (Ollie) have personally found that slowly scanning the class and saying to myself, 'on-task', 'on-task', 'off-task' to be particularly helpful. When a select few students are playing up, it can often feel like *all* students are playing up. This simple process helps to put the scale of student behaviour in perspective and to keep our eyes from frantically darting between those one, two, three, or four off-task students.

Plan your response	Plan to utilise one of the other scripts that you've prepared	It's likely that here you'll be utilising one of the other scripts that you've prepared (e.g. Routine 4: Gaining attention, or Routine 10: Moving a student). Or, if your video has helped you to identify a recurring pattern, you may want to specifically plan a script to respond to that pattern of student behaviour.
Deliberately practice	In the room that you teach in, decide where you will stand and rehearse out loud the exact words you will say in response to expected student misdemeanours. The more you automate your responses the more effectively and calmly you can respond to students in the classroom	Be as specific as possible. Use the names of students who are likely to misbehave. Predict their responses to your instructions. Plan responses to their responses! We can't plan for every situation but we can predict a high percentage of what will happen in class. Use video to help you spot behavioural patterns and to aid the planning process. Even better, get your colleagues to come in and play up, acting as your misbehaving students to practise in an even more realistic context.

What about when...?

#WAW: You're still feeling really stressed and triggered by the class		
Seek help personally and with the class	In some schools, even the most stoic teacher will struggle because behavioural norms of students are simply too bad, wild, or even abusive. In such cases, additional support is required. *'I'm finding the classroom behaviour of my year x's quite challenging. It's getting to a point where I get anxious thinking about them. Is it possible to have a chat?'*	Personal support: You may like to seek out support from a counsellor or psychologist to deal with personal regulation and emotional impacts of a disruptive class. Support with the class: It's okay if you need extra levels of support to work with a challenging student or class. This includes support from school leadership and school behavioural systems to manage behaviour effectively (see Routine 17: System Support). Ultimately, good behaviour is a whole-school project. If your school doesn't take behaviour seriously (including your safety and mental health), advocate for it, and/or look for a school that does!

#WAW: The class goes well		
Celebrate the small wins	If a class goes well, take a minute to enjoy your success: *I'd just like to say how well you focused today (or this first 15 mins). I could see you all trying hard and completing the work. Keep that up and we will have a great year.*	Teaching is hard and if you have a successful lesson or even part of a lesson, celebrate it! Then step back and see what it is that you might have done differently in this lesson that led to the positive result. Build on this success and celebrate the small wins. Mastering classroom management is an ongoing process, try to enjoy the challenge.

ROUTINE 4: GAINING ATTENTION

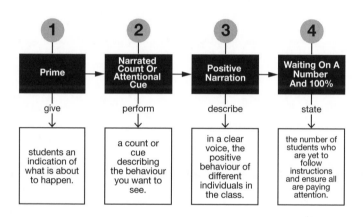

Students remember what they attend to.[47] If all students are listening to your explanations and thinking about the concepts, there is a greater likelihood they will learn them. If they're thinking about flicking another student with a rubber band, then that's what they'll remember. Quickly and efficiently gaining students' attention is the first step in the causal chain of learning.

47. Mccrea, P. (2017). *Memorable teaching: Leveraging memory to build deep and durable learning in the classroom.*

The routine

Gaining attention		
Tool	*Teacher talk* **and action**	**Notes**
1. Prime	*You have two minutes left to complete the starter.*	Move around the room. Also, give clear instructions for those who finish early.
	When you finish, open your books, write the learning intention, the date, then do some retrieval from your knowledge organiser until we begin instruction.	You can even put these instructions *on* the starter (or somewhere else visible) to help reinforce the expected routine.
2. Narrated count *or* **Attentional cue**	*Listening in 3,* *Pens down in 2,* *All eyes on me in… 1* Teacher: *One, two* Students: *Eyes on you*	Be descriptive with your narrated count, describing the desired action at each pause point. Especially for younger years, you can also use an attentional cue like: Teacher: *Tick tick* Students: *Boom* With older students, we've used the more age appropriate Teacher: *Founded in* Students: *'82* (school's founding date of 1882) Attention cues are also a great way to consistently reinforce school values. E.g., Teacher: *In our class* Students: *Punctual, polite, prepared*

3. Positive narration and if needed	Positive narration: *Angela has her pen down, Simon's eyes are on me, Eason is sitting up straight.*	Positive narration raises students' awareness to the desired behaviours whilst keeping all teacher talk positive.
proximity and if needed	Proximity: e. g., Move closer to more disruptive or less settled students.	Proximity is another great way to nip disruptions in the bud without explicitly correcting students.
non-verbals	Non-verbals: e.g. Finger to lips to quieten students, mime putting a pen down to remind a student to put their pen down.	Non-verbals correct behaviour whilst keeping the overall noise level low and avoiding announcing to the class that some students are off-task.
4. Waiting on a number and	*Waiting on two more students, now one more. Great. Let's get started.*	As the last student engages, wait 5-10 seconds for silence to let the energy in the room settle. Then start speaking in a quieter voice.
100%[48]	Wait till you have all eyes and ears before you begin. *We learn what we pay attention to. Listen to and think about what I am saying.*	Many students have implicitly learned that there is no real expectation for them to pay attention. Teach them that in your class, there is, and you won't start until you have 100% of students listening.

What about when…?

#WAW: Students forget equipment/ask to be excused during the transition to instructional phase		
Tool	*Teacher talk* and action	**Notes**
Pre-empt	*Put your hand up if you've forgotten a pen or paper, I'll let you borrow some from me and we can have a planning conversation at the end of class.*	It's useful to always have spare pens and paper to loan students. Make a note to retrieve them at the end of the lesson, and to have a planning discussion with the student.
Partial agreement	*Yes, you can go to the bathroom/get a drink, but let's just wait until after instruction. It's important that you follow this explanation so you're off to a good start.*	Use partial agreement to highlight the importance of attention during the instructional phase. Also, don't let students leave the room until they have demonstrated the skills or have started the work. Though temper this with professional judgement, compassion, and the sense of urgency and context of their request.

---

48. Lemov, D., (2010). *Teach like a champion: 49 techniques that put students on the path to college* (K-12). John Wiley & Sons.

ROUTINE 5: TIGHT TRANSITIONS

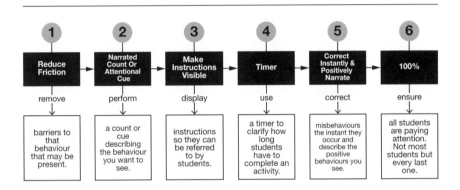

1	**2**	**3**	**4**	**5**	**6**
Reduce Friction	Narrated Count Or Attentional Cue	Make Instructions Visible	Timer	Correct Instantly & Positively Narrate	100%
remove	perform	display	use	correct	ensure
barriers to that behaviour that may be present.	a count or cue describing the behaviour you want to see.	instructions so they can be referred to by students.	a timer to clarify how long students have to complete an activity.	misbehaviours the instant they occur and describe the positive behaviours you see.	all students are paying attention. Not most students but every last one.

Guiding students to transition between different phases of a lesson is a natural part of teaching. In the classroom, this might mean transitioning through the following phases: entry routine, starter activity, instructional phase, independent work, and then to an additional activity or discussion. When done well, tight transitions facilitate the seamless movement from one activity to another, maximise learning time and reinforce a learning focus within your classroom. When done poorly, sloppy transitions can amount to weeks of lost learning time in a year.[49] To avoid this – and as a general rule – aim to spend less than 5% of lesson time on transitions (e.g. 3 minutes in a 60-minute lesson).

49. Lovell, O. (2022). *Tools for Teachers: How to teach, lead, and learn like the world's best educators*, John Catt Educational, pg. 93.

The routine

Tight transitions		
Tool	*Teacher talk* and action	Notes
1. Reduce friction	In a PE class: *Those behind the green cone, grab a green bib and move to the green square. Those behind the red cone, grab a red bib and move to the red square. For those behind the yellow cone, what do you think you'll do... Bilal?* Younger years: *As you enter the room you will be silent (voices off), collect your numeracy book and place it on your table. Then join me on the mat and be ready to listen.*	Make it as easy as possible. If students need materials, make sure they have them out during the entry routine. If they need to collect materials, locate them in an assembly line so there is 'one way' traffic. Having students put their books on their tables before you instruct reduces friction when you set them to work. You can even let students collect materials in small groups, e.g. *Front row, please go first and show us how it's done. Thanks front row, second row, your turn...*
2. Narrated count *or* **attentional cue**	*Listening in 3,* *Pens down in 2,* *All eyes on me in... 1* *Eyes this way,* *No talking,* *Nothing in your hand, thank you.*	Be descriptive with your narrated count, describing the desired action at each pause point. Especially for younger years, you can also use an attentional cue like: Teacher: *Tick tick* Students: *Boom* Or: Teacher: *1, 2, 3, eyes on me* Students: *1, 2, eyes on you*

3. Make instructions visible	E.g. ensure that the steps for the transition are written on the board. Or, in a practical in science or other subjects, ensure there's an image of each piece of equipment, or a sample work station with everything needed in clear view.	Visible instructions give you and the class something to point to, it saves you answering questions and adding to the noise level.
4. Timer	*We've got 60 seconds to do this. Begin when I start the timer… Go.*	The timer also helps to make expectations explicit. Students know what to do and how long they have to do it. This creates a sense of efficiency in the class.
5. Correct instantly and positively narrate	In a loud voice (not shouting) and usually only 2-5 seconds after you say go, you can add: *We forgot to do it quietly, sit down, let's try it again. This time when we get up, we will be quiet.* In a softer voice: *Now, quietly… Go.* Positively narrate (in a quiet voice): *Excellent work, that's much quieter.*	Similar to an entry routine, we need to correct instantly. If you hear chatter when you say 'go', call them out, ask them to sit down and do it again quietly.
6. 100%	*Thanks for putting your hand up, I'll answer your question shortly, I just need to make sure everyone has started. Read the instructions again and I'll be right with you.*	Your transition isn't complete until 100% of students have started the next task.

What about when…?

#WAW Your transition is complex		
Tool	*Teacher talk* and action	Notes
Use explicit instruction (see Routine 7)	*Okay PE class, three things before we get into the pool. You need to put your bags in the locker room, get changed into your swimmers and then sit on the far side of the pool.* *Point to the locker room for us… Al* *What do you need to get changed into… Seb?* *Where do you sit on the pool deck… Arav?*	For a complex transition, treat it like any other complex topic. Break it down into small steps, check for understanding after each step, then provide time for practice. It's okay to spend time in your first few lessons rehearsing the routine, this will save time in the long run.

#WAW Students are noisy during the transition		
Tool	*Teacher talk* and action	Notes
Reset	Stop the class with a clear: *Everyone stop and look this way in 3, eyes on me in 2, everything out of your hands in… 1. We forgot the silent part of the transition. Everyone back to your seats and we will have the chance to practise that again, I know you can do it well, let's have another go.*	Keep it positive and frame it as an opportunity to re-rehearse.

ROUTINE 6: AFTER CLASS CONVERSATION

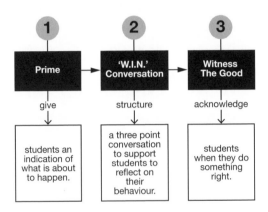

Even when we're using our tools and routines effectively, there will always be times when students don't meet our behavioural expectations. When we begin to see a pattern of poor behaviour in a student, or if there is an acute instance of poor behaviour in a lesson, it's important to have a follow-up conversation after class. This conversation has three objectives: 1. Provide an opportunity for the student to reflect on their behaviour, 2. Clarify the behavioural standard that needs to be met, and 3. Maintain the positive relationship between student and teacher and enhance the students' motivation to do better next time.

The routine

After class conversation		
Tool	*Teacher talk* and action	Notes
1. Prime	*Sofia, thanks for staying back. I'm keen for us to have a quick chat to make sure that we're on the same page and we have a positive start to the next lesson.*	Start with a positive message that conveys that the conversation is about forging a positive path forward together, rather than a lecture.
2. W.I.N. Conversation[50] What happened Impact	*To start off with, can you tell me **why** you think I've asked you to stay back today?* *What **impact** did that have?* (Students can reflect on the impact on *their learning* and on their *classmates' learning*) [Optional: *How does that relate to our school's values*] *What will you do **next time** you're in a similar situation?*	When a student says, *'I don't know'.* You can respond with, *'If you did know, what would you say'* or *'If you had to guess, what would you say?'* A reflection on impact acts as the impetus for behavioural change next lesson.
Next steps	*Is there anything I can do to support you to achieve this?*	Communicate that you are aiming to help the student meet the standard.
3. Witness the good	*Thanks Sofia. You've had a great start to the term and the way you helped Harry last lesson with his Cornell notes was fantastic. I know you want to do really well and today was just a little speed bump along the way. I'm looking forward to working with you tomorrow.*	Provides the student with a sense of positivity and helps them to see and feel that you believe in them.

---

50. The W.I.N. model was developed by the team at Brighton Grammar School, Melbourne.

What about when...?

#WAW: Student has a tendency to feel significant shame or become disheartened easily		
Tool	*Teacher talk* and action	Notes
Scaffold the conversation	Rather than asking the student the first two W.I.N. questions (what happened and what was the impact), briefly state these yourself, leaving space for the student to focus on the positive action moving forward. Avoid dwelling on or debating their transgression or mistake. W.I.N.: *In class today you called out three times during whole-class teaching time.* **(What)** *This interrupted my explanation, making it hard for other students to follow and impacting their learning.* **(Impact)** *What could you do* **next** *lesson during whole class teaching time that will lead to a better outcome?*	Students, and people more generally, habituate quickly to different types of interactions. If this is the first time a student has been in trouble, the conversation is likely to correct behaviour quickly. If a student is regularly in trouble and has heard this conversation many times, you may need to change it up to avoid them tuning out. Some alternative phrases could be: *I believe that you are a good person and want to do the right thing. What do you need from me to help you succeed?* Or *You worked well for 80% of that lesson, next time let's aim for 85% – I know you can do it.*

#WAW: Student responds to, or is likely to respond to, 'What happened?' with debate or denial		
Tool	*Teacher talk* and action	Notes
Partial agreement	Teacher: *Why might it be that I've kept you back for this chat Brooke?* Student: *I don't know, I didn't even start it, I was just trying to do my work and then Lorraine distracted me and started talking to me.* Teacher: *Lorraine may have started it, Brooke, I'm not sure. But for now, let's focus on what you can do next lesson to stay focused. What might you be able to say if Lorraine or another student does distract you during independent work time?* Student: *I don't know*	Partially agreeing with the student can enable the conversation to move swiftly on without entering any further into debate.
Model it	Teacher: *You could say something like, 'Please don't distract me, I need to do this work now so I don't have any homework tonight.'*	Students often don't have the conversational tools to communicate their needs to others. Modelling what a student can say can be the fastest way to give them these tools.
Rehearse it	Teacher: *I know you want to do well in this class. Do you think saying something like that might help both you and Lorraine to stay focused?* Student: *I guess so.* Teacher: *Great. You say it after me, 'Please don't distract me, I need to do this work now so I don't have any homework tonight.'* Student: *[Repeats]* Teacher: *Thanks Brooke, really looking forward to a focused lesson with you tomorrow. Enjoy your lunch.*	Just as practice helps teachers improve, it can also help students with their habitual behaviour. Don't be afraid to initiate practice if you feel it may help a student to respond productively next lesson. If students aren't doing the right thing in a situation it's often because they haven't been taught how.

#WAW: Students aren't changing their behaviour		
Tool	*Teacher talk* and action	**Notes**
Make instructions explicit	These conversations are for when the W.I.N. conversation isn't creating the change required. *Having a healthy relationship with rules is good for you and others. Rules exist so people can work together productively, and everyone benefits when they are followed. This is why people drive on the same side of the road, the rules are designed to keep everyone safe and help us all out.* *In life, we generally get what we give. If we're nice to someone else, they'll probably be nice back to us. In school, if we do something that others don't like, such as interrupting the learning of other students, the school will do something that we probably don't like too, such as enforcing consequences. This happens in life after school too, especially in our relationships. By knowing that you get what you give, you can take charge and give out positivity and helpfulness, and receive that from the world in return.* *…So, thinking about that, what might you do differently next time you are in class?*	There are several beliefs which, once gained, can help a student to better understand why appropriate behaviour is important and desirable. By explicitly sharing these ideas with students, we can help those who haven't picked them up already throughout life. Two of these ideas are:[51] Having a healthy relationship to rules is good for you and others. What you put out is what you get back.

---

51. Swann, R. (2023). Email to Mark Dowley, 16 June.

ROUTINE 7: EFFECTIVE INSTRUCTION 1 (I DO)

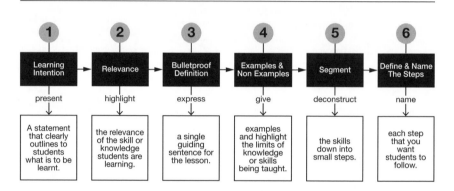

As we highlighted in Principle 7: Success is the greatest motivator. This means that often the key reason why a particular student is playing up in your lesson is because they aren't having success with the learning content. This suggests a simple solution… help them have more success! Explicit instruction is the fastest route to student success in relation to a wide variety of knowledge and skills, and explicit instruction often starts with a clear 'I do'. An 'I do' is the portion of the lesson in which the teacher clearly conveys and models the knowledge and skills students are to learn. This routine sketches the anatomy of an effective 'I do'.

The routine

Being a book focused on classroom management, rather than instruction, we have included the routine below as an introduction to effective explicit instruction. However, for a more comprehensive overview, see chapter 1 of Ollie's book *Tools for Teachers*.[52]

Effective instruction		
Tool	*Teacher talk* and action	Notes
Precede instruction with Routine 4 Gaining attention. Without all students' attention, learning cannot take place.		
1. Learning intention	*Students will learn to identify and describe the role of appositives in sentences.*	A learning intention tunes students into the core material to be learned and can provide initial exposure to new vocabulary and ideas.
2. Relevance	*Why are appositives important? Appositives help us to write interesting stories and texts that are both more informative, and more interesting for our audience.*	Briefly highlighting the relevance of the skill or knowledge that students are about to be taught can increase students' motivation to engage.
3. Bulletproof definition	*Appositive: A word or group of words that add detail to the noun that they follow.*	In a single sentence, a concise or 'bullet proof' definition captures the core knowledge that a student should take from a lesson or lesson segment.
4. Examples and non-examples	*Non-example without appositive:* Vanessa rode to school on a unicycle. *Example with appositive:* Vanessa, **who always wanted to impress the other children**, rode to school on a unicycle.	Provide students with models and worked examples of the skill you are trying to teach. This includes showing each step as well as the final output. Non-examples highlight the limits (i.e. boundary conditions) of the knowledge or skills being taught and can show what it looks like when they're not present.
5. Break skills down into small steps (Segment)	Ensure that each instructional segment limits the number of new pieces of information introduced to students at any one time	Students become overwhelmed when lots of information is presented at once. Segmenting instruction means that students don't get overwhelmed at any single point. Highlighting critical attributes allows students to make important connections between the big idea or process, and the constituent components that make up success.

---

52. www.ollielovell.com/t4t

| 6. Define and name the steps | *When you want to write an appositive yourself, follow these three steps:*

Step 1: <u>Identify the noun</u> that you want to provide more information about.

Step 2: <u>Draft the appositive</u>. It's a good idea to keep your appositive between around 3 and 7 words.

Step 3: <u>Put your appositive after the noun</u>, and place a comma at either end of the appositive to indicate pauses to the reader. | Breaking down your model for success into a few discrete steps makes it explicit to students exactly what they need to do to be successful. It also helps them to see how each action they take builds towards the overall picture.

Naming the steps (underlined left) provides a quick way for the teacher to refer to each step during both the instruction, and the feedback phases of a lesson. |

What about when...?

#WAW: Dealing with disruptions during instruction		
Tool	*Teacher talk* and action	Notes
Non-verbal	Hand signals to indicate *open your books, shh, eyes this way* encourage the correct behaviour.	Make eye contact and correct with as little interruption to the class as possible.
Self-interrupt	*Okay, today we are going to learn how to...* [pause – wait for the off-task student to look at you]*... write a topic sentence.*	Use once or twice during an instruction. After that, escalate to describe and direct.
Describe and direct	*Anita, you are talking, attention this way thanks.*	Sometimes it's okay to skip this step and go straight to directed choice.
Directed choice	*That's twice now that you've spoken during instruction time, you can choose to stop talking or you'll need to sit up front to focus.*	Use this early, particularly in your first class. Set the standard that when you talk, students listen.

#WAW: Student asks an irrelevant question		
Tool	*Teacher talk* and action	Notes
Authentic acknowledgement	*Thanks for your initiative in asking that question Priya, that is a very interesting question but the answer will take us slightly off track so let's save that one for a few minutes until everyone is on track then you and I can have a brief chat about it.*	Some valuable things to acknowledge are effort, attention, engagement, initiative, or courage. You can then choose to redirect *I'm keen for us all to stay on these three steps now. Thanks though.* Or, you could delay (as modelled in the script left.)

ROUTINE 8: EFFECTIVE INSTRUCTION 2 (WE DO)

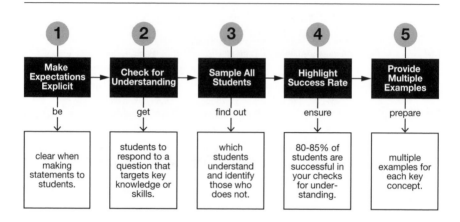

1	2	3	4	5
Make Expectations Explicit	**Check for Understanding**	**Sample All Students**	**Highlight Success Rate**	**Provide Multiple Examples**
be	get	find out	ensure	prepare
clear when making statements to students.	students to respond to a question that targets key knowledge or skills.	which students understand and identify those who does not.	80-85% of students are successful in your checks for under-standing.	multiple examples for each key concept.

The goal of 'We do' is to check that students understand the skill they are learning. It also supports the efficient transition from teacher-led instruction to independent practice. Often, straight after teacher modelling, students aren't yet ready to fully take on a task for themselves. This is where the 'We do' comes in. The key to a successful 'We do' is for the entirety of the task to be broken down into bite-sized chunks and for the teacher to check for student understanding and accuracy after each chunk.

The routine

Note: As with Routine 7: Effective instruction (I do), the table below is complemented by chapter 1 of Ollie's book, *Tools for Teachers*.[53]

We do		
Tool	*Teacher talk* and action	Notes
1. Make expectations explicit	*Choral response, on my signal.* Or *Have your mini-whiteboards ready. Remember: Write big so I can read it and hover* till I say show me.* Or *Now write the answer in your book now.*	Within a We do, it's imperative to have a mechanism for checking for understanding from all students after each small chunk of instruction. Choral response is effective when done well, finger voting (with heads down so students don't influence each other's answers) works for multiple-choice questions. Mini whiteboards are perhaps the most versatile tool for this when the response is short and concise. To make this run smoothly, you will need to be explicit about how you want students to respond, and to also practise this response method with your class over time. *Students 'hover' by holding their whiteboards upside down and ready to show the teacher. This both shows the teacher who is ready and reduces the chances of students copying each other's answers.
2. Check for understanding	*3, 2, 1, show me.*	Students hold their whiteboard so you can see all responses.
3. Sample all students	*I'm waiting for two more whiteboards. Keep them up till I say 'down' thanks.*	Ensure that you're basing your understanding of competence on responses from all students.
4. High success rate	*Excellent work, almost everyone has it, and I know who to help during independent work time.* [Begin the transition to independent work routine.]	The question you pose to students should be very similar to your example. Often 80-85% accurate responses is the target, but as close to 100% as possible is better. A useful way to think about the target success rate is as follows: How many individual students are yet to be successful, and can you practically support them all during independent work time? If you can make it to them all, it's ok to begin independent work. If not, you may need to engage in another batch of whole-class instruction then roll out another 'We do' to obtain a higher initial success rate amongst the class.

53. www.ollielovell.com/t4t

5. Provide multiple examples	*Great, I can see that a high percentage of our class have this right. Let's do one more as a group to really make sure we can nail it before independent practice.*	Preparing for class by preparing multiple 'We dos' allows you to teach responsively within the lesson and to continue with instruction, or transition students to independent work, as needed.

What about when…?

#WAW: Student have specific learning needs or individual learning plans		
Tool	*Teacher talk* and action	Notes
This is an excerpt from a learning profile, created by a psychologist for a neurodivergent student: ■ provide a seating plan to ensure she is at the front ■ minimise distractions ■ explicit clear instructions for tasks and classroom routines ■ dual coding (visual/verbal) ■ check in for understanding ■ clear guidelines and deadlines for assessment tasks	*We will have a seating plan for the first four weeks. It will give you a chance to meet someone new but will also help me to learn your names.* *When I teach, I promise I'll break skills down into small steps to make it easier for you. What I need from you is to silently pay attention and complete the 'We do'. If you do that, I guarantee we will all learn a lot this year.*	All students benefit from clear routines and instruction. Breaking down skills into small steps, providing practice after each step and checking for understanding supports all learners. The best thing we can do for students with additional needs [for those who don't require additional specialist support] is provide them with a calm, quiet and engaged classroom with high quality instruction. Clear expectations and consistent routines minimise distractions and support learning.

ROUTINE 9: MONITORING BEHAVIOUR DURING INDEPENDENT WORK

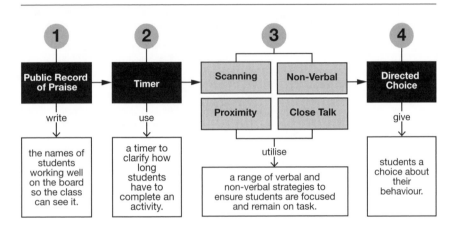

Students working quietly and independently is a common sign of a productive classroom. This is the phase in which students undertake the deliberate practice required to encode core content into long-term memory. The aim during this phase is to keep students focused on the work and the learning while minimising common disruptions such as talking or avoiding work. A teacher's role is to monitor behaviour and give students support in their learning in the most efficient way possible.

The routine

Note: The tools provided below need not be used in sequence. Rather, they are more of a set of options for you to choose from depending upon your context and preferences.

Monitor behaviour during independent work		
Tool	*Teacher talk* and action	**Notes**
[Precede this lesson phase with Routine 5: Tight transitions]		
Public record of praise	[On board] *Fast starters:* *Jude* *Casper* *Bianca* *Quyen* *Amy*	Recording 'fast starters' or 'focused work' (or any other category you see fit) can be a positive way to reinforce and acknowledge positive behaviour. It can be good to limit the list to five or so students each time, otherwise they can overly focus on getting their names on the board. You can also refer to portions of the room, e.g. 'Whole back row', etc.
Timer	*You have 15 minutes to silently get as much done as you can. I'll start the timer now. Go!*	Making independent practice time-bound (and ensuring that the timer is clear and visible) is incredibly effective for helping students to stay focused. If they are struggling with their behaviour, knowing that there's only 6 minutes and 48 seconds left of silent work can help them to regulate themselves more effectively. It also provides a clear delineation of this portion of the lesson. When the timer is on, students know they must be in focused work mode.
Scanning	Stand in the front corner of the room. Hands together, craning neck (but in a relaxed and expectant manner), exaggerating that you are looking for who is working.	You'll find students regularly look up from their work to see what the teacher is doing. Acknowledging them with an encouraging smile and nod will refocus them.
Proximity	Move quietly to any place you see students off-task.	Physical presence often has a powerful influence. You need to do little more than simply move into the off-task students' proximity. Your seating plan should make this easier.

Non-verbal	Some options: Touch a student's book to indicate for them to continue working. Mime the process of writing to refocus a student.	Develop your own non-verbal signals that you use consistently with students to communicate key expectations to them.
Close talk (with describe and direct)	*Luke, you have completed two questions in the last ten minutes. When I come back in two minutes, I expect at least two more questions to be completed. You can do it, thanks.*	If the previous steps don't work, move close to the off-task student and address them in a quiet voice. A quiet and discrete correction can stop it from becoming a distracting incident for other students. Take up time: *When I come back in two minutes…* avoids a standoff and makes expectations explicit. End with *thank you*, not *please*, to communicate your implicit expectation that they will comply with your request.
Directed choice	[Can also be used following the 'Close talk' script above] *Luke, you can either finish the next two questions or I'll need to move you to somewhere you can focus better. Your choice.* To escalate: *Luke, if you choose to keep talking, we'll need to have a discussion with your head of house/year/parents. You decide what happens next.*	If this follows an initial warning, it can be effective to give a consequence (such as a sanction straight away) and to make the consequence of the directed choice a step up from that.

What about when...?

#WAW: Students ask for help before 100% of students have started		
Tool	*Teacher talk* and action	Notes
Partial agreement	*Yes, I'll answer your question. I just need to make sure everyone has started before I get to you. Read the question again and see if you can start. I'll be with you once everyone is working quietly.* *Give me one moment Casey till everyone's settled* [shorter version of the above]. *Yes, you can get a drink/go to the bathroom, just answer the first three questions so I know you've got this, then you can go.*	Highlight the collective nature of the classroom. If you have lots of questions from students, you probably need to return to the instructional phase and address students' challenges (and pre-empt these questions next time). If a student goes to the toilet before they have practised and consolidated the skill, it is highly likely they will forget it by the time they return.

#WAW: Multiple students make low level disruptions or noise		
Tool	*Teacher talk* and action	Notes
Describe and direct	*I'm hearing some noises from the back right corner* [gesture to the area], *settling into this work now, thank you.*	Be calm. Often these noises are designed to get a reaction from the teacher.
Directed choice	*There are still noises coming from this back right corner. If you choose to keep making them, I'll keep this group of students* [gesture to area] *back to sort it out. I don't expect it will come to that because you are mature enough to be quiet. Thank you.*	Portray a sense of calm expectancy. Act as if you have it all under control and have dealt with this type of behaviour before.
Enforce consequence	*You've chosen to keep making the noises, the names here* [written on board] *will stay back after class so that we can make a plan for a more productive lesson next time.*	Send the message of *I care about your learning and this is why I have high standards. I expect better because you (as a class) can be better. I've seen it and I believe in you.*

#WAW: There is an interruption (visitor to class, movement outside, etc.)		
Tool	*Teacher talk* and action	Notes
Describe and direct	*There is a distraction outside and I can see we're all curious. Let's take a look for ten seconds then we're going to refocus. Look now, 10, 9, 8, ... 3, 2, 1.* [Use Routine 4: Gaining attention]. *Excellent, let's continue our work now, thank you.*	It's natural for students, particularly younger students, to get distracted by interesting things outside the class. Acknowledge it and, if appropriate, give students an opportunity to satiate their curiosity before supporting them to refocus.

#WAW: Something inappropriate happens (sexist, racist, physical violence)		
Tool	*Teacher talk* and action	Notes
Describe and direct	*That is sexist/racist/violent language, we don't accept that in this classroom. Step outside please and I will come and talk to you. Thank you.* (Use Routine 2: Defuse debate as required.)	Use a louder voice so the class can hear you. Be calm and direct. Note that we've identified the language or action as being sexist/racist/violent, not the student. It's depersonalised. This way our follow up conversation can be about the language or action, not the individual.
Restate calmly	*If other students laugh/comment, say:* That behaviour is not acceptable in this class and I wouldn't expect anyone in here to find that funny. I'll follow up with the student on the consequences. Quietly back to work now. Thank you.[54] *Emily – if you choose to keep laughing, you'll need to step outside to calm down for a minute.*	Use once or twice during an instruction. After that, escalate to directed choice: *You can choose to get back to work or you can wait outside for the consequences.* If something funny happens and students can't control themselves, you can politely ask them to step outside.

---

54. Thanks to Bill Rogers in particular for his modelling of this phrase in *Education Research Reading Room Podcast* episode #31: https://www.ollielovell.com/billrogers/.

ROUTINE 10: MOVING A STUDENT

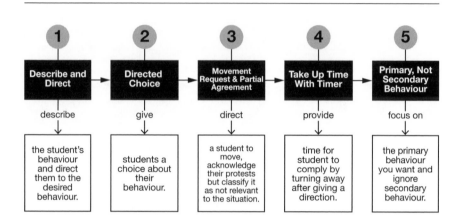

Despite our proactive planning, misconduct will likely still occur at times so it is best to prepare for this and have routines for dealing with it. If a student is regularly misbehaving, (talking, not completing work, and so on) and their location in the classroom is contributing to that, moving them to another part of the room is a useful strategy. Moving a student sends a clear message about your high expectations of the class. The aim is to minimise disruptions and maximise learning time for students.

The routine

Moving a student		
Tool	*Teacher talk* and action	Notes
1. Describe and direct	*Miriam, you are talking, work silently so that you and others can make the most of your learning time, thank you.*	Be clear. It can be helpful to add a brief comment on the 'why' (... make the most of your learning time) too.
2. Directed choice	*Miriam, you can choose to either work quietly where you are or move to the front of the room. It's up to you.*	The word 'choose' is important, it allows the student to take ownership of their own behaviour and of the decision to refocus.
3. Movement request + partial agreement	[If student continues to talk] *Miriam, you are still talking, pick up your books and move to the seat at the front, thank you.* Miriam: *I'll stop now, I promise, just let me stay here.* *Maybe you will, but you chose to keep talking so you'll need to move up the front now, thank you.* [Turn away and address another student to give a small amount of take up time.]	A clear and firm directive sends the message to this student, and others, that expectations will be upheld in this class. Avoid bargaining as it will encourage other students to bargain with your requests.
4. Take up time (with timer)	[If student still hasn't moved, or started moving, within a reasonable time frame.] *Miriam, you have one minute and by the end of that minute I expect you to be in the front seat. Thank you. Your time starts... now.* [Turn and walk away, set a timer or mime that you are.]	Turning and walking away breaks the standoff and debate that's occurring between student and teacher and signals to them that the discussion is over and the decision is final. If the student hasn't moved after this, you need to escalate the issue to a higher level of management as the student is willfully not complying with a reasonable request. This follow up can happen immediately, or after class, pending your school's systems.

| 5. Primary, not secondary behaviour | [Ignore any minor pouting, sighing, mumbling under the breath, slamming of books that the student may engage in. If you need to, follow up at the end of class.]

Use #WAW in Routine 9 for when 'something inappropriate happens'.

Finally, once a student has moved and is on-task. Witness the good by saying *I can see you working quietly now, well done. Keep it up.* | If other students say, *Did you see/hear that, miss?* Defuse this with: *Thanks for your support, but monitoring behaviour is my job, thanks Stacey.*

If the secondary behaviour is extreme (e.g. throwing a chair). Escalate using system support (Routine 18). |

What about when…?

#WAW: Students flat out refuse		
Tool	*Teacher talk* and action	Notes
Directed choice	*You can choose to move now, or we can follow this up after class – your choice.* Or *You don't have to move, but if you choose not to, I'll need to let your parents and head of house know about this. Your call.*	If other students see the blatant refusal and comment, *He still hasn't moved, miss,* just say, *It's under control, Henry made his choice I will follow up with his head of house/year level coordinator later, back to your work now, thanks.*

#WAW: Multiple students are talking/misbehaving		
Tool	*Teacher talk* and action	Notes
Describe and direct	*I'm hearing a lot of talk from these three students. If the people in this area aren't quiet, I'll move one of you.* [After continual disruption] *You have continued to talk. Sandra, up the front, thanks.* Sandra: *That's not fair.* *Maybe not, you're the person moving now, and I'll be monitoring the other two as well. Thanks Sandra.*	Often moving the middle student of three is effective as it creates space.

ROUTINE 11: COMPLEX ACTIVITIES

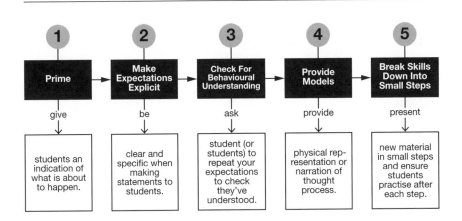

Often classroom management will be going very well. That is, however, until you try to do some sort of complex activity like group work, a class discussion, lab work, or a practical in class. As soon as students are invited to contribute, collaborate and participate with others, this can lead to behavioural challenges. However, it doesn't have to be this way. To be successful, teachers need to model the new behaviours students are required to demonstrate and back this up with structure and support. A useful way to conceptualise this is that you need to explicitly teach students what you want them to do *and* how you want them to do it.

The routine

Complex activities		
Tool	*Teacher talk* and action	Notes
1. Prime	*Eyes on me and listening thanks. Today we are going to be doing something different that requires a bit more interaction for you all. It's an opportunity to demonstrate your people skills and ability to work with others. I only do this with classes I trust, but I think you are ready for it. Give me a nod if you think you are.*	Set the scene that you expect them to do well. Expect the best and narrate this to students.
2. Make expectations explicit	*There are three expectations: 1. Be kind, 2. Listen to each other, 3. Share thoughtfully.*	Hold up three fingers to indicate the three requirements.
3. Check for behavioural understanding	*What's the first expectation* [pause], *Harry?*	Repeat for the other two instructions.
4. Provide models	**Example 1: Class discussion** Teacher: *For class discussions, here are some sentence structures you might want to use. I'll be listening to see who uses good structures in our discussion.* *– Building on ...'s point, I'd like to add...* *– I agree with ... in that. But I disagree that ... because ...* *– I'd like to contest ...'s claim that ... because ...* **Example 2: Group work** Teacher: *Here are some phrases that you can use during group work:* *We haven't heard from ... for a while. What do you think ...* *Let's go around and hear from everyone briefly before we decide what to do* *There seems to be a bit of disagreement. Let's come back to our main goal. Which of these approaches is most likely to get us there and why?* *Does everybody feel like they have a role and know what to do in the next 10 minutes?*	Students often haven't participated in effective classroom discussions, we need to explicitly teach them the skills required. Have these up on the board too for student reference. Working as a team is a skill and can be explicitly taught, we can't expect students to already have these skills.

5. Break skills down into small steps	In complex activities, clearly define and scaffold each step in the activity and set a time limit. This allows students to follow the process.	Avoid asking students to 'research' during class time. Unless you are explicitly teaching research skills. The cognitive load is high when students need to learn how to research and learn the new content at the same time.

What about when...?

#WAW: Students are off-task/the activity isn't working		
Directed choice (to the class)	Use Routine 4: Gaining attention, then: *Okay class, we've been working on this for 10 minutes and the noise level is too loud. Let's all go quiet for a moment [Pause for 5-10 seconds]. We can either do this activity properly, or we will go back to working from the textbook. I'll repeat the instructions and I know we can do better this time.*	Complex activities required a new skill set for many students. Be prepared for them to make mistakes and correct them.

ROUTINE 12: MAINTAINING ENGAGEMENT TILL THE END OF THE LESSON

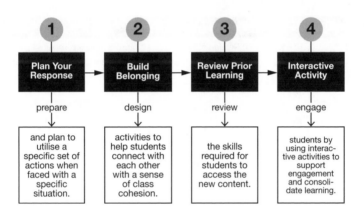

Timing can be difficult to manage during a class. We suggest using the previous routines to maintain engagement for as long as possible. You might occasionally find the engagement in the class begins to wane towards the end of a period. When this happens, it's useful to have some tools and routines to maintain engagement.

The routine

Note: The tools provided below need not be used in sequence. Rather, they are more of a set of options for you to choose from depending upon your context and preferences.

Maintaining engagement to the end of the lesson		
Tool	*Teacher talk* and action	Notes
Plan your response	Quiz *For those finishing early, we have a review quiz for you to complete. It should take ten minutes and give you a chance to retrieve the key skills for this unit. Complete it silently, thanks.*	It's worthwhile always having a back-up quiz on you as a teacher. It's a useful task that can provide a productive finish to a lesson. If you don't have a quiz, you can write questions on the board and ask students to complete them as an exit ticket. This is also a powerful Formative Assessment strategy that can inform your planning for the next lesson
Build belonging	*Okay students, finish the question you are on and close your books.* *The next few minutes we are going to do something different. I'm going to ask a question and you will have a short, quiet conversation with someone you don't know that well as yet. When the timer stops, you stop talking and listen to the next question.* Example questions: *- What do you enjoy doing outside of school and why?* *- If you could travel to any place in the world, where would it be and why?* *- What are your plans for the upcoming weekend?*	This helps students get to know each other. We are sacrificing learning time but it's a useful strategy to help students connect. The more they connect the more likely they are to work well together. The idea underpinning this is 'finding common ground'. It's a way to build belonging and connection within a group. This tool is particularly useful at the start of a new year with students. This is likely a time when they are still building and regaining their stamina for independent work (after the holidays), and when they may not know each other that well as of yet. Consider your context, if students already know each other well, this probably isn't the best choice. If students don't know each other's names and are shy to speak up in front of the class, it can be a great strategy to use.

Review prior learning	This can be a next step following the 'build belonging' discussion approach. Putting students into new partnerships then providing them with reflection questions can get them talking and interacting, as well as cementing learning. Some good questions can be: *Define, in your own words…* (prior concept). *What is the main thing you will take away from today's lesson?* *What is one thing you don't yet understand from* (this lesson, last lesson, last week, etc)? *What was one bit of feedback that you received in your last assessment that you are currently working on?*	Reflecting on and sharing about learning that has occurred, as well as areas for improvement, is a method of retrieval and can help to clarify and consolidate prior learning.
Interactive activity	*Well done team. We hit our goal of 20 minutes of silent and focused work so let's finish off with a quick retrieval race to close the lesson.* *Let's split the class down the middle. This is Team A and this is Team B.* *I'm going to ask a question and I want you to either remember, look through your notes to find the answer, or quietly share it with your partner. The first side with all hands up I'll cold call someone to answer and if they get it right, that team gets the point.* *Ready? Here we go…*	Select interactive activities that can support learning *and* engagement. You can use a retrieval game such as the game described left, or a digital alternative such as Kahoot!, Quizizz, Quizlet Live or Gimkit.

ROUTINE 13: ASKING A STUDENT TO PICK UP RUBBISH

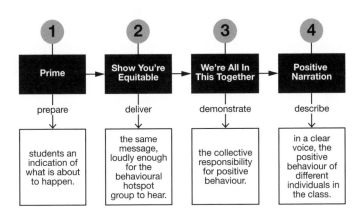

A great school has high behavioural expectations both inside and outside of the classroom. Maintaining a clean and orderly environment supports students to feel safe and valued wherever they are in the school. By asking students to pick up rubbish, we show them that they deserve a pleasant area to play and socialise in and demonstrates our shared responsibility for care of the school.

The routine[55]

Asking students to pick up rubbish		
Tool	*Teacher talk* and action	**Notes**
1. Prime	*Good morning. Please make sure you clean up all the rubbish in this area before you leave, even if it's not yours, thank you.*	Identify potential behavioural hotspots in the yard and try to address the students in that area at the start of break time before any issues arise, such as these students leaving rubbish behind at the end of break.
		The key line in the script to the left is 'even if it's not yours'. This pre-empts the likely excuse that students will give at a future time when you do ask them to pick up that rubbish.
		You can add additional messaging before the 'thanks' such as, *'We all have a role to play in keeping the school clean.'* (Or a similar point, especially if it's in line with a whole-school narrative.)
		Ensure you deliver this request with a smile.
2. Show you're equitable	Go to the group of students next to the behavioural hotspot group and deliver exactly the same message, loudly enough for the first group to hear you!	This step is absolutely key. It suggests to the first group (the behavioural issue hotspot group) that you weren't targeting or picking on them. Instead, you're just going around reminding students of a standard expectation of being in the playground.
3. We're all in this together	Once it does come time to ask students to pick up some rubbish.	The positive assumptions at the start of this script ('it's probably not yours') is key, as it avoids a debate about whose rubbish it is or isn't.
	I know it's probably not your rubbish, but could you help keep the school looking great by picking up that juice box and wrapper? I'll get this foil. Thanks. (Then bend down and pick up a piece yourself).	Show you care about the environment through leading by example during the clean-up too. Again, use whole-school messaging if possible. Whole-school language around clean and safe environments, or respecting the learning environment, or looking after nature, and so on, can be powerful.
4. Positive narration	*Thanks for picking that up, Marco, very helpful.*	If you see a student picking up rubbish without prompting, you may even have a quiet word to their home room teacher/year level coordinator to help reinforce this great behaviour.

---

55. Routine 13 draws heavily on the advice and guidance of Bryn Humberstone. A big thanks to Bryn for his deep insight and generous sharing in this space.

ROUTINE 14: ADDRESSING A UNIFORM INFRACTION

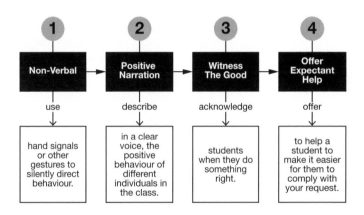

Uniform is another outside-the-classroom area that can be challenging to enforce. This can be especially tricky because often you do not have an existing relationship with the student whose uniform you need to correct. It's helpful to keep in mind that monitoring uniform standards in the yard is not only an opportunity for student corrections, it can also be a time and place where you begin to bank positivity and build relationships with students. This routine is aimed to do just that.

The routine[56]

Addressing a uniform infraction		
Tool	*Teacher talk* and action	Notes
1. Non-verbal	Smile, nod, and gesture to the uniform correction (e.g. mime tucking in your shirt).	A non-verbal gesture for a uniform infraction is the least invasive way to correct student behaviour.
		Make sure you smile whilst doing this, and nod or mouth 'thank you' at the end to show that you implicitly expect compliance.
2. Positive narration	*Look at that beautifully tucked in shirt, Thao. You're looking ready to learn!*	Often you do not need to address a student directly in order for them to correct their uniform. Instead, you can identify a student next to or near them who is doing the right thing and audibly acknowledge this person. This can boost uniform compliance of the target student whilst keeping all messaging positive.
		This can be done with or without knowing the partner's name too (e.g. 'Beautifully tucked in shirt.'). You can also ask their name afterwards ('What is your name?', 'Thao', 'You're looking ready to learn Thao!')
3. Witness the good	*Loving that tucked in shirt today Avery. Looking very smart.*	If you asked Avery to tuck in their shirt yesterday, acknowledge that it's done without prompting today.
		This can also be done non-verbally. A gesture, then a thumbs up and nod can work wonders.
4. Offer expectant help	*Good morning, Harry. Would you like me to hold your toastie whilst you take that (non-school) jumper off?*	This strategy is fun and powerful. It communicates both that you're willing to help the student and it also suggests the benefit of the doubt by implying, 'I know you would have taken that jumper off if only your hands weren't full. Let me help you.'
		It's very hard for a student to refuse your generous offer for help!

---

56. Routine 14 draws heavily on the advice and guidance of Bryn Humberstone. A big thanks to Bryn for his deep insight and generous sharing in this space.

What about when…?

#WAW: A student won't comply with your uniform request		
Tool	*Teacher talk* and action	Notes
Directed choice	*You can choose to keep the jumper on but if you do, I'll need to let your parents and head of house know about this. Your call.* *It's under control. Julian made his choice and we will follow up with head of house/year level coordinator and parents later.*	This is another form of the routine for 'blatantly refusing'. If other students see the blatant refusal and comment.

ROUTINE 15: ADDRESSING ROUGH OR INAPPROPRIATE PLAY

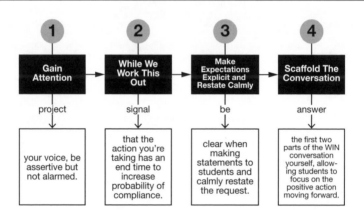

Rough or inappropriate play is a clear no-no. However, even though it can be dangerous, the way that you deal with it doesn't need to be too iron-fisted. The approach in this routine is designed to help you to defuse potentially dangerous play in a way that assumes the best and leaves students with a clear plan of what to do next time. The specific scenario here is students tackling in a non-tackling zone (which is likely your whole playground).

The routine[57]

Addressing rough or inappropriate play		
Tool	*Teacher talk* and action	Notes
1. Gain attention	Teacher: *Hey all, stop. What are we doing?*	Project your voice; be assertive but not alarming. Questions are not usually recommended in behaviour management (as they can invite debate), but when you are trying to gain student attention, they can be a helpful way to initiate engagement.
2. While we work this out	Student (who was tackling another student): *He took my ball so I'm getting it back!* Teacher: *I'll hold the ball whilst we work this out…*	Taking the ball gives you immediate control of the situation. Framing it like this (I'll take the ball whilst we work out what's happening) increases the likelihood that students will hand over the ball because you've put an end date on it. There is also the implicit message to students that if you can't work it out, the ball will be retained by you.
3. Make expectations explicit and restate calmly	Teacher: *This is a quiet space, no ball games here.* Student: *We were just playing, miss.* Teacher: *Maybe so, but this is a quiet space, no ball games.*	Clearly state the expectation. Ideally, frame it in the positive, reinforcing whole-school language and messaging where appropriate.

---

57. Routine 15 draws heavily on the advice and guidance of Bryn Humberstone. A big thanks to Bryn for his deep insight and generous sharing in this space.

4. Scaffold the conversation	Teacher: *So what could you do next time someone takes your ball off you?*	Help students to plan what to do next time.
	Student: *Ask nicely.*	
	Teacher: *And did you try that?*	Ask if they have or did try that.
	Student: *I did, but he didn't give it back.*	
	Teacher: *And then what other options might you have? What about the presence of me as a nearby teacher?*	Point out to them alternate options.
	Student: *Oh yeah, I guess I could ask you.*	
	Teacher: *Fantastic, great plan. Enjoy the rest of your lunch, that was a fantastic header you did before Chris!*	Finish on a positive note.

ROUTINE 16: CLEARING THE YARD

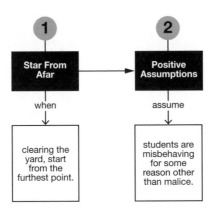

Clearing the yard at the end of break time, and hurrying students off to class, can be a big challenge when they may be absorbed in their games and, let's face it, not in any hurry to get to class at all! Here are two quick techniques to support you to do this.

The routine

Clearing the yard		
Tool	*Teacher talk* and action	Notes
1. Start from afar	Begin clearing the yard from the farthest point from your target destination. For example, if all students must exit the field through the north gate, start encouraging those students at the southmost end first.	Starting from the furthest point means that as students begin to move, they implicitly encourage all students in front of them to begin moving towards the exit too. This harnesses a social norm to help clear the field. Conversely, if you try to convince the student next to the gate to move first, you'll find yourself having 100 little conversations trying to get students out. And the most stubborn students (who may purposefully position themselves as far away from the gate as possible) will still be playing. Other students will look around and think, 'Well, those students are still playing, so I can too'.
2. Positive assumptions	*It's pretty loud out here, so you might not have heard, but the bell just went. Off to class now. Thank you.*	Communicate to students that you are giving them the benefit of the doubt and simply issuing a helpful reminder in case they didn't hear the bell.

What about when…?

#WAW: Students keep shooting the ball		
Tool	*Teacher talk* and action	Notes
3. Directed choice	*You can have your final shot and go inside, otherwise you can give the ball to me to hold, your call.*	Students always want one last shot, giving one student the extra five seconds to take it and then leave often makes the transition back to class smoother.

ROUTINE 17: STUDENTS USING TECHNOLOGY IN AN UNPRODUCTIVE WAY

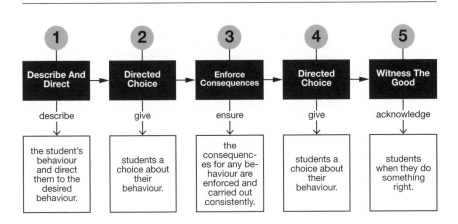

The distractions inherent in technology limit students' ability to pay attention. This means that if students have access to a phone, iPad or laptop with notifications that distract them, they are less likely to learn. We strongly encourage a school-wide rule of 'no phones in class'. This routine gives an example of how to draw from your repertoire of tools to manage a student who refuses to give up their phone.

The routine

Students using technology in an unproductive way		
Tool	*Teacher talk* and action	**Notes**
1. Describe and direct	Teacher: *Kaevish, you are on your phone. Put it away and focus on your work, thanks.* Student: *I was just texting my mum ...*	Be as succinct as possible in your language. Expect a counter response from students.
2. Directed choice	Teacher: *Maybe so* (partial agreement), *but we have a school rule about phones. You can put it away or put it on my desk. The choice is yours (allow take up time).* Student puts phone away ... 60 seconds later ... Student starts looking at phone again.	Respond to any pushback in a way that doesn't escalate the discussion. By saying '*we have a school rule*' you can depersonalise the correction. Whole-school rules are not up for negotiation and therefore you and the student are both responsible for upholding the standards of the school.
3. Enforce consequences	Teacher: *I gave you the choice. Put your phone on my desk now, thanks. You'll get it back at the end of the lesson.* Student: *Puts phone away but doesn't follow your instruction.*	Always enforce consequences in a calm way.
4. Directed choice	Teacher: *You can either put it on my desk now, or we can have a longer conversation after class with you, me and the head of house/year. Your choice.* Student: *Mutters, curses under their breath, has a big sigh and drags their feet to the front of the class.*	Use the same tool of directed choice but with more serious consequences.
5. Witness the good	Teacher: *Great decision. I'll pop back in a moment to see how you're getting on and if there's anything I can help with.*	Tactically ignore the secondary behaviour (sighing, pouting, slamming books), focus on getting the student quiet and learning. End with a supportive comment.

What about when…?

#WAW Students deny any wrongdoing		
Tool	*Teacher talk* and action	Notes
Restate calmly	Student: *I wasn't looking at my phone.* Teacher: *You had the choice earlier and you made it. Phone on my desk now thanks. You'll get it back. I'll give you 30 seconds to make sure it's on silent and on my desk. It's distracting you from your work. Thank you.*	Expect a response from the student and use your self-regulation skills (Routine 3) to stay calm and respond.

#WAW Students challenge your authority		
Tool	*Teacher talk* and action	Notes
Partial agreement and restate calmly	Student: *You can't make me give up my phone. It's mine.* Teacher: *Maybe not, but I can ask you again to choose between putting it on my desk now, or having a discussion with the head of house after class. I know you'll make a good decision.*	Avoid a direct power battle with the student. Ending with the positive 'I know you'll make a good decision' lets the student know you believe in them.

#WAW Students attempt to bargain		
Tool	*Teacher talk* and action	Notes
Restate calmly	Student: *No, I promise I'll put it away, please give me one more chance…* Teacher: *The choice was very clear and you chose to use your phone. On my desk thanks, you'll get it back at the end of class.*	Avoid debating or bargaining with a student. It sets an undesirable precedent

ROUTINE 18: SYSTEM LEVEL SUPPORT

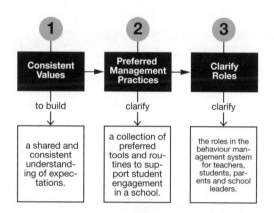

Schools need to provide the conditions that allow a teacher to be successful. This includes having school values and clear standards linked to them. The school leadership must clarify their preferred behaviour management strategies (tools and routines) and also provide support for teachers to track and escalate inappropriate student behaviour. A full description of system level support is beyond the scope of this book, but this section highlights the role of the school in supporting teachers to manage the classroom.

The routine

System-level support		
Tool	*Teacher talk* and action	Notes
Consistent values	*Gordon, we don't talk to each other like that. That behaviour doesn't align with our school value of respect.* Or... *One of our values as a school is accountability. Part of that means completing all the set work. We can stay back for five minutes and you can finish those questions.*	School values give teachers something to reference when they are speaking with students. They are the 'givens' that come with being part of the community. When a school has consistent values, teachers can use these in their scripts with students to both reinforce school values, and draw on shared messaging. The more teachers use the values, the easier it is for students to remember and understand them.
Preferred management practices (tools)	Examples of these tools can be found in this book. Proximity: [Move closer to more disruptive or less settled students]. Directed choice: You can get back to work now, or you can sit up front with me. Your call.	A school needs to clearly describe their preferred management practices and give teachers time to learn and practise them. Consistency in management practices decreases variability between teachers and makes it easier for teachers and students. A full description of each tool within this book can be found in the glossary.
Clarify roles	Roles of teachers and schools need to be clarified. This includes preferred practices (key tools and routines, W.I.N. conversations), system support (tracking system, clear escalation system), and opportunities to learn and practise management skills (professional learning).	The school is responsible for clarifying practices, providing system support and creating opportunities to learn and practise behaviour management skills. The teacher is responsible for using the preferred management practices, following school processes and upholding consistent standards.
Harness social norms	If students are exhibiting a behaviour that is below the standard you expect, for example; teasing, making silly sounds in class, not sharing equipment, a useful phrase to use is a simple *'We don't do that here'.*	Teachers need an opportunity to discuss and unpack school expectations. This means clarifying standards of behaviour, uniform, engagement and conduct. E.g. *'What do you do when students are late?'* is a question worth discussing. This can take significant professional learning time, plus periodic reminders and reinforcement for staff, but is essential for consistency and impact.

Low hanging fruit	*Katie, the last few lessons you have been a bit disruptive. I know that Simon caused the initial disruption and I'll follow up with him. But I want you to focus on your behaviour now. You are usually really focused on your work so let's build on that and I'm keen to see you back to your focused self next lesson.*	Research suggests that if *more* than 10% of a classroom is disruptive, a teacher can spend up to 25% of their time trying to get things under control, instead of focusing on learning. Conversely, if *less* than 10% of the class is disruptive, the time spent managing drops to 10%.[58] This often means that even if we don't manage to fully address the behaviour at the extremes (e.g. your most disruptive student), if we help those students on the borderline (e.g. those who need a nudge in the right direction to be engaged) to make changes, this can cause significant shifts in the classroom.
Record keeping	Teachers need a way to record student misbehaviour that is fast and easily accessible. Many excellent digital solutions exist that also streamline aggregation and reporting. Short of that, we recommend having a hard copy of the seating plan at hand on a clipboard. If students misbehave, you can write a short note (or a symbol) next to their name, e.g 'calling out'.	The purpose of record keeping is to ensure that repeated, low level behaviour is corrected. This will feed into a system where a group of teachers have oversight and can take action to correct behaviour. After class, you can use your notes to feed accumulated positive and negative student behaviour into the appropriate whole-school system.
Repeated minor indiscretions	Often schools wait until a major incident (fight, drugs, abuse of teacher) to apply major consequences (suspension/expulsion). We argue that repeated low level behaviours should have the same consequences.	Schools need to avoid scenarios where students are consistently 'just below' the acceptable standard. Repeated low-level behaviours systematically erode the learning culture within a school and can have significantly negative long-term effects. For this reason, we must take repeated low-level behaviour seriously.
Escalation	Sometimes students repeat unacceptable behaviour and consistently choose not to make the most of the learning opportunities presented to them. When this happens across multiple classrooms, escalation is required.	A clear system of how to escalate behaviour problems, enlist support from parents and provide further opportunities needs to be designed and communicated to all stakeholders. An example of such a process is detailed on the next page.

58. Goss, P., & Sonnemann, J. (2017). *Engaging students: Creating classrooms that improve learning.* Grattan Institute.

Example of a behavioural process[59]

Level 1: Minor behaviour infringements are managed using tools and routines in the classroom.

Level 2: Repeated, low level unacceptable behaviour including:

- Repeatedly disrupting the learning of others.

- Repeatedly not following classroom expectations.

- Repeatedly arriving late or not ready to learn.

- Off-task comments during instruction or independent work time or acting disrespectfully to others.

Teacher action: Have a conversation (e.g. W.I.N. Framework) and record in a school-wide system.

Level 3: After three conversations are logged, student to meet with the head of house/year level coordinator. After the first meeting, the parents can be informed. For a second or third meeting, parents can be involved. Supports and strategies are put in place to help build the student's awareness of their behaviour and give them positive coping strategies. Rehearsal of strategy use for a student can also be crucial here.

Level 4: After three meetings with the head of house/year level coordinator, the student is escalated to the school leader. Positive coping and behavioural strategies are clarified and reinforced. Further rehearsal of strategy use is imperative.

Level 5: If, after meeting with the school leader, there is no positive behaviour change, the students' place at the school can be seriously reconsidered.

---

59. This behavioural process is adapted from Brighton Grammar School, Melbourne.

What about when…?

#WAW: Your school doesn't have clear behaviour support structures		
Tool	*Teacher talk* and action	Notes
Build them or go elsewhere	It is near impossible to be a successful teacher in a school without supportive systems. We encourage you to either build them quickly or find a new school.	Please do feel free to reach out if you're keen to discuss what this could look like in your context.

CONCLUSION

Students' engagement in the classroom is a crucial foundation for their engagement in life itself. This book set out to synthesise the key principles of behaviour management and present to you the tools and routines required to create the calm and productive environment that all students and teachers deserve.

From the vast expanse of literature that delves into behaviour management, it was a huge challenge to distil the most practical and high-impact teaching strategies and present them in an accessible manner. We chose the final set of ideas presented within these pages because we have seen them work with teachers and students in a diverse range of contexts. Importantly, we use these strategies every day in our own classrooms.

Education is a fundamental human right. By showing your dedication and making it to the end of this book, you have made an impactful contribution to granting that human right to more students, in more classrooms. We hope that you feel the weight of this impact now and in the years to come as you use these tools, scripts and routines time and time again.

We hope that you enter your next class with a smile on your face, with a renewed sense of excitement, and with a deeper confidence in your abilities to scaffold impactful learning for every moment of your lesson. Remember that, beyond a shadow of a doubt, the work you undertake each and every day truly matters. We are with you on this journey. So, get out there, get practising and good luck.

If you would like to share any stories or feedback on your experience in using these routines. Please visit us at www.classroommanagementhandbook.com.

APPENDICES

Appendix 1: Glossary of tools

Tool	Definition	Found in routine #	Found in #WAW
100%	Make sure that all students are paying attention; not most students but every last one.	4, 5	
Attentional cue	A cue or routine used to quickly and efficiently gain attention, e.g. Teacher: *1, 2…* Student: Eyes on you.	4, 5	
Authentic acknowledgement	Warmly acknowledge positive behaviours from a student (effort, attention, initiative).		7
Break skills down into small steps	Present new material in small steps and ensure students practise after each step.	7, 11	8
Build belonging	Activities to help students connect with each other and with the sense of the class as a cohesive unit.	12	
Build them or go elsewhere	Create behaviour management systems in your context or find a school that has them.	18	18
Bulletproof definition	Core knowledge expressed in a single sentence that can act as a guiding filter for planning a lesson or set of activities.	7	
Celebrate the small wins	Congratulate the class when they do well for a lesson or part thereof.		3
Check for behavioural understanding	Ask a student (or students) to repeat your expectations to check they've understood.	11,1	
Checks for Understanding	During the instructional phase, check that students have understood the concept by having them to respond to a question that targets key knowledge or skills.	8	5

Clarify roles	Clarity the roles in the behaviour management system for teachers, students, parents and school leaders.	18	
Close talk	A quiet comment to a student to refocus, usually the volume of a whisper.	9	
Consistent values	School values give teacher something to reference when speaking with students to build a shared and consistent understanding of expectations.	18	
Correct instantly	Correct any misbehaviours the instant they occur. Particularly valuable for transitioning to independent work.	5	
Define and name the steps	Name each step that you want students to follow, both behaviourally and during instruction. This makes the steps clear and more memorable.	7	
Deliberately practice	In the room you teach (where possible), rehearse, out loud, the exact words you will say and the actions you will take as if it's the real deal! This helps build habits of effective instruction.	3	
Describe and direct	If a student is off-task, describe their behaviour and direct them to the desired behaviour. Teacher: *You are out of your seat, sit down and focus on your work, thanks.*	7, 9, 10, 17	7, 9, 10
Directed choice	Give students a choice about their behaviour. Teacher: *You can be quiet and focus on your work or you can move to another seat in the room, your choice.*	2, 7, 9, 10, 17	2, 7, 9, 10, 11, 13, 14, 16
Do it again	Invite students to repeat an activity. Every student is held to the standard and is expected to do it again, until it is correct.	1	
Enforce consequences	Ensure the consequences for any behaviour are enforced and carried out consistently. Do so in a positive way.	17	9
Escalation	A system for progressively increasing the consequences of students' actions as their actions become more severe.	18	
Harnessing social norms	Use common standards of expected behaviour to influence others to conform to those standards.	18	
High success rate	Ensure 80–85% of students are successful in your checks for understanding (but 100% is better!) before you progress to the next part of the lesson.	8	

Interactive activity	Use interactive activities to support engagement and consolidate learning.	12	
Learning intention	A statement that clearly outlines to students what is to be learned.	7	
Low hanging fruit	Addressing behaviour by focusing first on the students on the borderline of acceptable behaviour, rather than the most challenging students.	18	
Make expectations explicit	Be clear when making statements to students. *Listen up is not clear. Eyes on me, lips sealed talking, listening to the instructions* is easier for students to understand.	1, 8, 11	1
Make instructions visible	Displaying instructions on the board or projector so they can be referred to by students.	5	
Model it	Model the behaviour you expect from students.		6
Movement request	A clear and firm direction to ask a student to move.	10	
Narrated count	A count with descriptions of behaviour, e.g. *Listening in 3, pens down, 2, all eyes on me in... 1.*	4, 5	
Non-examples	Non-examples highlight the limits (aka: boundary conditions) of the knowledge or skills being taught.	7	1
Non-verbal	Use hand signals or other gestures to silently direct behaviour, e.g. *finger to lips* for silence, *palms open* for open books.	4, 9, 14	7
Offer expectant help	Offer to help a student to make it easier for them to comply with your request.	15	
Partial agreement	A statement that acknowledges a students' protest but classifies it as not relevant to the current situation, e.g. Student: *Everyone else was talking.* Teacher: *Maybe they were, but I'm asking you to focus on your work now. Thanks.*	10, 17	4, 9, 17
Plan your regulation	Have an internal routine to regulate your emotions, e.g. stand tall, take a deep breath, smile, repeat a positive mantra to yourself.	3	
Plan your response	Prepare and plan to utilise a specific set of actions when faced with a specific situation.	3, 12	
Positive assumption	Assume students are misbehaving for some reason other than malice (e.g. forgetfulness, instructions insufficiently clear, etc).	16	

Positive narration	Describe, in a clear voice, the positive behaviour of different individuals in the class. This raises the attention of other students to the expectation and builds positive norms.	1, 4, 13, 14	
Pre-empt	Plan for common challenges that occur in the classroom.		4
Preferred management practices	A collection of preferred tools and routines to support student engagement in a school.	18	
Primary, not secondary behaviour	Focus on the primary behaviour you want from students. Ignore secondary behaviour such as pouting, sighing, slamming books, etc.	10	
Prime	Give students an indication of what is about to happen.	1, 4, 6, 11, 13	
Provide models	Models can be physical representations of completed tasks (paragraph), conceptual models (e.g. behaviour of particles in a solid, liquid or gas) or a narration of thought processes.	11	
Provide multiple examples	Prepare multiple examples for each key concept.	8	
Proximity	If students are off-task, physically moving near them and not saying anything is often enough for them to refocus.	4, 9, 18	
Public record of praise	Write the names of students working well on the board (or use another similar system) so the class can see it.	9	
Record keeping	A way to record behaviour in the class to ensure repeated, low-level behaviour is corrected.	18	
Reduce friction	Make it as easy as possible for students to complete a desired behaviour by removing any barriers to that behaviour that may be present.	5	
Rehearse it	Give students an opportunity to practise behaviours and phrases.		6
Relevance	Highlighting the relevance of the skill or knowledge students are learning.	7	
Repeated minor indiscretions	Treat repeated minor incidents as serious behaviour incidents and apply the appropriate consequences.	18	

Reset	Stop the class during the activity and restate the expectations and instructions.		5
Restate calmly	If a student argues or talks back, calmly restate the request.	2, 9, 15	9, 17
Review prior learning	Review the skills required for students to access the new content.	12	
Sample all students	When students respond (e.g. using mini-whiteboards) make sure you know who understands and who does not.	8	
Scaffold the conversation	Answer the first two parts of the W.I.N. conversation yourself, allowing students to focus on the positive action moving forward.	15	6
Scanning	Be intentional about how to scan a classroom. Look for the engagement of students and the quality of their work.	9	
Seating plan	The teacher chooses where students sit to maximise engagement and minimise disruptions.		1
Seek help personally and with the class	If the need arises, don't hesitate to seek out professional support either personally (counsellor) or with a colleague within the school.		3
Segment and highlight critical attributes	Break instructions down and make a point of highlighting critical ideas and connections.	7	
Self-interrupt	Interrupt your own statement to highlight to students that you expect them to behave prior to you continuing.		2, 7
Start from afar	When clearing the yard, start from the furthest point.	16	
Take up time	After giving a direction, turn away from the student and give them some time to comply. This avoids an ego-driven stand-off that can sometimes follow a request.	10, 2	2
Threshold	Meet students at the door and set positive expectations before they enter the room.	1	
Timer	Use a timer to clarify how long students have to complete an activity.	5, 9, 10	

Video	Filming yourself teaching, and your students, can provide a great way to more objectively see what is occurring in your classroom.	3	
W. I. N. conversation	A structured conversation to support students to reflect on their behaviour. It consists of three key points: 1. What happened, 2. What was the impact? 3. Next steps to make this right...	6	
Waiting on a number	Describe the number of students who are yet to follow instructions, e.g., 'I'm waiting on three people'.	4	
While we work this out	A way to signal that the action that you're taking (e.g., taking a ball from a student) has an end time, thereby increasing the probability of the student complying.	15	
Witness the good	Catch students when they're doing the right thing and acknowledge it. This builds relationships and positively weights the ratio of acknowledgements to corrections with each student.	6, 14, 17	

Appendix 2: Further reading

The journey to behaviour management mastery is long but rewarding. Once you have mastered the tools and routines in this book, we encourage you to delve deeper into the behavioural management literature. The following five books are a treasure trove of useful information about how to help students be engaged in learning.

Further reading

You Know the Fair Rule: Strategies for positive and effective behaviour management and discipline in schools by Bill Rogers (2011; Australian Council for Educational Research).

Teach Like a Champion 3.0: 63 Techniques that Put Students on the Path to College by Doug Lemov (2011; John Wiley & Sons).

Tools for Teachers: How to teach, lead, and learn like the world's best educators by Oliver Lovell (2022; John Catt Educational).

Running the Room: The Teacher's Guide to Behaviour by Tom Bennett (2020; John Catt Educational).